S0-AHG-574

WITHDRAWN

Biography Today

Profiles of People of Interest to Young Readers

Volume 18
Issue 3
September 2009

Cherie D. Abbey
Managing Editor

Omnigraphics

P.O. Box 31-1640
Detroit, MI 48231

Cherie D. Abbey, *Managing Editor*

Brian Baughan, Peggy Daniels, Kevin Hillstrom, Laurie Hillstrom, and Diane Telgen,
Sketch Writers

Allison A. Beckett and Mary Butler, *Research Staff*

* * *

Peter E. Ruffner, *Publisher*
Matthew P. Barbour, *Senior Vice President*

* * *

Elizabeth Collins, *Research and Permissions Coordinator*
Kevin M. Hayes, *Operations Manager*
Cherry Stockdale, *Permissions Assistant*

Shirley Amore, Martha Johns, and Kirk Kauffman, *Administrative Staff*

Special thanks to Frederick G. Ruffner for creating this series.

Copyright © 2009 EBSCO Publishing, Inc.
ISSN 1058-2347 • ISBN 978-0-7808-1052-5

Library of Congress Cataloging-in-Publication Data

All rights reserved. No part of this publication may be reproduced or transmitted in any form or by any means, electronic or mechanical, including photocopy, recording, or any information storage and retrieval system, without permission in writing from the publisher.

The information in this publication was compiled from sources cited and from sources considered reliable. While every possible effort has been made to ensure reliability, the publisher will not assume liability for damages caused by inaccuracies in the data, and makes no warranty, express or implied, on the accuracy of the information contained herein.

This book is printed on acid-free paper meeting the ANSI Z39.48 Standard. The infinity symbol that appears above indicates that the paper in this book meets that standard.

Printed in the United States

WITHDRAWN

Contents

Preface

Biography Today is a magazine designed and written for the young reader—ages 9 and above—and covers individuals that librarians and teachers tell us that young people want to know about most: entertainers, athletes, writers, illustrators, cartoonists, and political leaders.

The Plan of the Work

The publication was especially created to appeal to young readers in a format they can enjoy reading and readily understand. Each issue contains approximately 10 sketches arranged alphabetically. Each entry provides at least one picture of the individual profiled, and bold-faced rubrics lead the reader to information on birth, youth, early memories, education, first jobs, marriage and family, career highlights, memorable experiences, hobbies, and honors and awards. Each of the entries ends with a list of easily accessible sources designed to lead the student to further reading on the individual and a current address. Retrospective entries are also included, written to provide a perspective on the individual's entire career.

Biographies are prepared by Omnigraphics editors after extensive research, utilizing the most current materials available. Those sources that are generally available to students appear in the list of further reading at the end of the sketch.

Indexes

Cumulative indexes are an important component of *Biography Today*. Each issue of the *Biography Today* General Series includes a Cumulative Names Index, which comprises all individuals profiled in *Biography Today* since the series began in 1992. In addition, we compile three other indexes: the Cumulative General Index, Places of Birth Index, and Birthday Index. See our web site, www.biographytoday.com, for these three indexes, along with the Names Index. All *Biography Today* indexes are cumulative, including all individuals profiled in both the General Series and the Subject Series.

Our Advisors

This series was reviewed by an Advisory Board comprising librarians, children's literature specialists, and reading instructors to ensure that the concept of this publication—to provide a readable and accessible biographical magazine for young readers—was on target. They evaluated the title as it developed, and their suggestions have proved invaluable. Any errors, however, are ours alone. We'd like to list the Advisory Board members, and to thank them for their efforts.

Gail Beaver
Adjunct Lecturer
University of Michigan
Ann Arbor, MI

Cindy Cares
Youth Services Librarian
Southfield Public Library
Southfield, MI

Carol A. Doll
School of Information Science and Policy
University of Albany, SUNY
Albany, NY

Kathleen Hayes-Parvin
Language Arts Teacher
Birney Middle School
Southfield, MI

Karen Imarisio
Assistant Head of Adult Services
Bloomfield Twp. Public Library
Bloomfield Hills, MI

Rosemary Orlando
Director
St. Clair Shores Public Library
St. Clair Shores, MI

Our Advisory Board stressed to us that we should not shy away from controversial or unconventional people in our profiles, and we have tried to follow their advice. The Advisory Board also mentioned that the sketches might be useful in reluctant reader and adult literacy programs, and we would value any comments librarians might have about the suitability of our magazine for those purposes.

Your Comments Are Welcome

Our goal is to be accurate and up-to-date, to give young readers information they can learn from and enjoy. Now we want to know what you think. Take a look at this issue of *Biography Today*, on approval, and send me your comments. We want to provide an excellent source of biographical information for young people. Let us know how you think we're doing.

Cherie Abbey
Managing Editor, *Biography Today*
Omnigraphics, Inc.
P.O. Box 31-1640
Detroit, MI 48231-1640
www.omnigraphics.com
editorial@omnigraphics.com

Congratulations!

Congratulations to the following individuals and libraries who are receiving a free copy of *Biography Today,* Vol. 18, No. 3, for suggesting people who appear in this issue.

Alexis, Groveport, OH

Carol Arnold, Hoopeston Public Library, Hoopeston, IL

Judi Chelekis, Vassar High School Library, Vassar, MI

Ashley Daly, Ardmore High School, Ardmore, AL

Liz Keaton, Columbus, TN

A. Kennedy, Ardmore High School, Ardmore, AL

Andrea Lopez, Oxnard, CA

Shreya Subramanian, Martell Elementary School, Troy, MI

Christy Zhao, Brooklyn, NY

Will Allen 1949-

American Urban Farmer and Activist
Pioneer in the Development of Community-Based
Urban Farming

BIRTH

William Edward Allen was born on February 8, 1949, to Willie Mae and O.W. Allen. His mother worked as a housekeeper, and his father was a former sharecropper. The second youngest of seven kids, Allen grew up on a farm in Rockville, Maryland, outside Washington DC. His parents had purchased the farm after moving from South Carolina.

YOUTH

As a boy, Allen had plenty of farming chores. He learned early on that farming was physically demanding yet rewarding work. He and his siblings would put in long hours tilling the soil and pulling weeds. Come harvest time, they enjoyed the fruits of all their labor. The farm produced 85 percent of the food the family ate, and Allen enjoyed his share. "There was always food on the stove. And Willie ate more than anybody," his older brother Joe remembered.

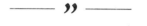

> "My parents were the biggest influence on my life," said Allen. "We didn't have a TV and we relied on a wood stove, but we were known as the 'food family' because we had so much food."

The Allens didn't live in luxury, but Willie Mae and O.W. provided their children with plenty of guidance and other essentials. "My parents were the biggest influence on my life," said Allen. "We didn't have a TV and we relied on a wood stove, but we were known as the 'food family' because we had so much food."

When Allen was 13, he started playing basketball. He wasn't an all-star right away, but he knew that he could build on his athleticism and his size. "I could run like a deer, and I was really strong," he said. He was also dedicated to improving his game. He even fashioned a makeshift court by flattening out some ground on the farm and hanging a bushel basket on an oak tree. By pointing a flashlight at the basket, he ensured that he could play into the evening.

EDUCATION

The late-night sessions served Allen well as he continued to improve and grow taller. While attending Julius West Junior High in Rockville, he became the star of the eighth-grade team. Rival teams feared him as the only player who could dunk the ball. By the time he began playing for Richard Montgomery High School, he towered over most players, standing at six feet seven inches tall and weighing 230 pounds.

When Allen was only a sophomore, the *Washington Post* selected him for the All-Metropolitan team, placing him among the best-ranked players in Washington DC and surrounding counties. In 1966, his junior year, Allen led his team to win the Maryland state championship. His squad lost in the state finals the following year, but he was selected for the All-American team, one of the highest distinctions in high school athletics. He also received a scholarship to play for the University of Miami in Coral Gables, Florida.

Allen majored in physical education at the University of Miami, and he made school history as the Hurricanes' first African-American basketball player. He attended college during the late 1960s, a time of deep divisions in race relations in the United States. Allen even received death letters from Ku Klux Klan members, showing that some Floridians had no tolerance for black athletes playing for the university. But Ron Godfrey, the coach at the time, saw a determination in Allen that helped him handle opponents on and off the court. "He put his heart and soul into everything he did," Godfrey said, "and encouraged other young black players to come to Miami at a time when schools were just integrating."

Along with excelling on the court, Allen also proved he was an activist who could rally support for a cause. During his junior season, the school's Board of Trustees issued a sudden announcement that it was about to cancel the basketball program, which spelled disaster for the players since they did not have enough time to transfer to another school. Allen quickly organized his teammates to wage a player strike and hold a press conference. The campaign attracted the attention of the national press, which forced the Board to extend the basketball program for another year. Allen was thus able to play in his senior year. He graduated from the University of Miami in 1971.

CAREER HIGHLIGHTS

Playing Professional Basketball

Allen left college prepared for a bright future. Not only was he on track to play basketball professionally, but he was also married already. He had met his wife, Cynthia, early in his college years, and they were married on February 8, 1969.

Allen was drafted to play for the Baltimore Bullets (the former name of the Washington Wizards), but he quickly transferred to the Miami Floridians, a team that was part of the short-lived American Basketball Association. After finishing the 1971-1972 season with the Floridians, Allen decided to play with the European Professional League.

While living in Belgium and playing in the European Professional League, Allen made friends with some local farmers. He found that the more time

*Allen developed a love of farming as a child
and then returned to that early love as an adult.*

he spent with them, the more they brought him back to his family roots. "They farmed a lot like we used to," Allen recalled. "It must have released a hidden passion in me, because before I left Belgium, I had a garden and some chickens of my own."

In 1977, Allen ended his basketball career and returned to the United States. By that time he and Cynthia were the parents of three children under the age of eight: Erika, Jason, and then Adriana. Allen and the family settled in Cynthia's hometown of Milwaukee, Wisconsin, where some of her family lived.

Allen took a series of full-time jobs, first as an executive at Marcus Corp. and then as a technology salesperson for Procter & Gamble. The work paid well, but over time farming became more attractive to him. "I needed the farm—it's so real and so satisfying," he said. "Mostly, I wanted that life for my kids."

Preserving the Family Farming Legacy

In 1982, Allen quit his job at Procter & Gamble and picked up the vocation he had forsaken years ago. "I remember when I left for Coral Gables, telling my father, 'I will never work on a farm again.' I guess you should never say never." With money from a hefty settlement package with Procter & Gamble, he bought a junkyard tractor and 100 acres of land in Oak Creek, a suburb south of Milwaukee.

Using the sales skills he acquired during his corporate career, Allen sold his vegetables at local markets. He also asked his kids to work on the farm, just as his father did with him. It wasn't a rich life, but by preserving the legacy of the older generation, Allen and his family were learning self-reliance—and enjoying all the good food that came with it. Erika remembered, "My dad would always say, 'You'll thank me someday 'cause you know how to work and grow food.'"

> *While living in Belgium and playing in the European Professional League, Allen made friends with some local farmers. He found that the more time he spent with them, the more they brought him back to his family roots. "They farmed a lot like we used to," Allen recalled. "It must have released a hidden passion in me, because before I left Belgium, I had a garden and some chickens of my own."*

Nine years into his new enterprise, Allen was eager to expand his operations. He set his sights on a two-acre parcel of land on the north side of Milwaukee. The plot was on a busy street, making it an optimal spot for business. Allen was also happy to know he was saving what was the last remaining farmland in the city, in a low-income neighborhood that was once known for its agricultural activities but now provided minimal access to healthy, affordable food.

Settling in what was once called Greenhouse Alley, he constructed a greenhouse of his own. Will's Roadside Stand soon became a popular stop for organic produce. During that time he also established the Rainbow Grower's Cooperative, which connected family farmers outside Milwaukee to consumers in the city.

Soon, Allen was receiving several requests for help to start up gardening projects. In 1995 a group from a nearby YWCA came to him for ideas on how neighborhood youths could make a small organic garden profitable. He offered them a one-half acre of unused land behind his greenhouse. The kids got to work and soon were producing a healthy crop. Having the children nearby provided an opportunity for Allen to do some mentoring.

"I talked to them about how the garden was teaching basic life skills: how to get up in the morning, how to be responsible for growing something," he said.

Developing a Nonprofit Farming Group

An idea for a nonprofit organization began forming in discussions between Allen and other local urban farming enthusiasts with whom he begun partnering. He was certain he wanted to use sustainable practices to grow crops and distribute them in what he calls "food deserts," urban areas where there is plenty of junk food for sale but not much affordable produce. He also wanted his organization to include a mentoring program for Milwaukee's youth. Finally, no matter what, his collaborators got a clear message that he needed his approach to remain hands-on. "I told them the only thing I wanted to do was to have my hands in the soil and help teach these kids," he said.

Allen started mentoring the kids who came to his farm. "I talked to them about how the garden was teaching basic life skills: how to get up in the morning, how to be responsible for growing something," he said.

Under Allen's leadership, Farm City Link formed in 1995. A year later, he was approached by Heifer Project International, a charitable organization that helps to relieve hunger through old and new agricultural techniques. The Heifer Project had several ideas on how Farm City Link could expand its operations, including setting up a fish farm of 150 tilapia; bringing in a large supply of red worms to enrich the soil of the vegetable beds; and implementing a hydroponics system, which uses a nutrient-rich solution to grow plants in water. Allen eagerly used all of Heifer Project's ideas at Farm City Link.

In those first years, Farm City Link struggled financially. One of the major challenges for Allen was figuring out how to grow a large amount of crops in the facility's tight quarters, which, along with the raised vegetable beds had to make room for chickens, ducks, goats, and farmed fish. He also felt divided between remaining productive and keeping his commitment to training new farmers. Those concerns were addressed in 1998, when he met Hope Finkelstein. An organizer and activist, Finkelstein had recently formed Growing Power, a nonprofit group with a similar focus. Impressed

When children got involved at the farm, Allen's role grew to include mentorship.

with Farm City Link's work, Finkelstein suggested they increase their capacity by merging the two organizations, with Allen as co-director.

Allen agreed wholeheartedly with the proposal. He immediately identified with the name Growing Power, which aligned with his goal to "grow communities by growing sustainable food sources." In 1999, the building once known as Will's Roadside Stand became Growing Power's Community Food Center, where farmers young and old received training and assistance in farming practices.

The group's mission became to support people from diverse backgrounds by providing equal access to healthy, high-quality, safe and affordable food. To reach this goal, Growing Power provides hands-on training, on-the-ground demonstrations, outreach, and technical assistance—all with the goal of helping people grow, process, market, and distribute food in a sustainable manner. According to the group's web site, "Our goal is a simple one: to grow food, to grow minds, and to grow community. Growing Power began with a farmer, a plot of land, and a core group of dedicated young people. Today, our love of the land and our dedication to sharing knowledge is changing lives."

Involving kids in the farming community is an important part of the Growing Power mission. The organization promotes the Growing Power Youth Corps, a youth development apprenticeship program that gives academic and professional experience to kids from low-income backgrounds. Kids in the Youth Corps can learn about different farming methods, develop leadership experience, build entrepreneurial skills, and learn to work with diverse groups of people.

Branching Out

As Allen's vision became a reality in Milwaukee, he and his organization decided to start another program in a nearby city. Growing Power selected Chicago for the new program and asked Allen's eldest daughter, Erika, to lead it. Now an adult and an art teacher, Erika had a special bond with kids, along with plenty of farming know-how. The new branch opened in February 2002 and began establishing more Community Food Centers. From the beginning, Allen showed confidence that his daughter could handle the challenges of the job. "People admire Erika's intelligence and grasp," he said. "But her commitment and passion are incredible, and that's what it really takes."

> "Will Allen is an urban farmer who is transforming the cultivation, production, and delivery of healthy foods to underserved, urban populations," according to the award statement from the John D. and Catherine T. MacArthur Foundation. "Allen is experimenting with new and creative ways to improve the diet and health of the urban poor."

In 2002 the Growing Power farm was producing over 100,000 pounds of chemical-free vegetables and continually adding more staff and volunteers to its operations. To remain productive, Allen needed to locate more funding, and he did that in 2005 when he won the Ford Foundation Leadership for a Changing World Award, which included a $100,000 grant from the Ford Foundation.

Three years later, in 2008, Allen received the highly prestigious "genius grant" from the John D. and Catherine T. MacArthur Foundation. The $500,000 award for MacArthur Fellows is presented to "individuals across all ages and fields who show exceptional merit and promise of continued creative work." In the award statement, the organization said that "Will

The Growing Power Youth Corps is an apprenticeship program that involves neighborhood kids in farming, entrepreneurship, and leadership activities.

Allen is an urban farmer who is transforming the cultivation, production, and delivery of healthy foods to underserved, urban populations.... Allen is experimenting with new and creative ways to improve the diet and health of the urban poor." To Allen, the award helped signify that public attitudes about his line of work were dramatically changing. "I think it's really a recognition that will really help push this movement forward so people start eating healthier," he said.

News of Allen's award led to a string of interviews with "Good Morning America," CNN, National Public Radio, and the *New York Times*. By that time, Growing Power had literally gone global. Over the course of distant travels, Allen had conducted trainings in Africa, Europe, and South America. The Growing Power headquarters had become massive, now with three dozen full-time employees working in five large greenhouses and annually producing half a million dollars worth of fresh, organic food. Now the leader of a large organization, Allen could still experience the simple joy of getting kids excited about farming. "You just see the enthusiasm in the young people grow right along with the tomatoes and peppers," he said.

17

Future Plans

Allen's enterprises have been ambitious thus far, but his future ideas for Growing Power could surpass them all. His dream for the main facility includes a five-story, glass-walled building that would act as a vertical farm. Allen and other pioneers see vertical farming as a powerful solution to today's challenges of large-scale agriculture. Like the present facility, the building would devote resources to farming instruction. "Three-fourths of the building would be used for growing, and the other part would be classrooms for teaching," he explained.

As wild as Allen's idea sounds, he has the support of the organization. Said Growing Power board president Jerome Kaufman: "Yes, it will be a major shift. But Will is an innovator. He has started new ventures. He has done this all of his career."

Now the leader of a large organization, Allen could still experience the simple joy of getting kids excited about farming. "You just see the enthusiasm in the young people grow right along with the tomatoes and peppers," he said.

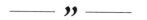

MARRIAGE AND FAMILY

Allen has been married to his wife Cynthia for over 40 years. They have three children: their daughter Erika works for Growing Power; their son Jason is a lawyer; and their daughter Adriana is a model/actress.

Of the three children, Allen spends the most time with Erika since they work together. "I had my kids when I was very young, so I grew up with them," he explained. "But we've made that transformation from father/daughter to friends.... Now it's more equal." In collaborating with and teaching Erika what he knows, Allen knows she will in turn pass on the tradition to other farmers. As she explained, "I have that legacy—that generational appreciation—because my dad sacrificed so much of his time to develop something."

HOBBIES AND OTHER INTERESTS

Because Growing Power has become such a large organization, serving as its director takes up most of Allen's time. He does, however, set aside time to watch basketball. He sometimes flies down to the University of Miami to attend home games at his alma mater. An enthusiastic eater and cook,

Allen also will stop his work routine to fix a tasty meal for his employees using ingredients from Growing Power's greenhouses.

HONORS AND AWARDS

Leadership for a Changing World Award (Ford Foundation): 2005
Macarthur Fellowship Award (Macarthur Foundation): 2008

FURTHER READING

Periodicals

Better Homes and Gardens, Summer 2007, p.64
Christian Science Monitor, Jan. 29, 2009, p.17
Madison Capital Times, Sep. 25, 2008
Milwaukee Journal Sentinel, Apr. 19, 2008; Sep. 23, 2008; Oct. 6, 2008; Jan. 27, 2009
Money, Sep. 2002, p.30
New York Times, Oct. 1, 2008, p.6
Yes! Magazine, Spring 2009

Online Articles

http://www.biztimes.com
   (Biztimes, "Growing Power: The Farm in the City," May 30, 2008)
http://www.macfound.org
   (The John D. and Catherine T. MacArthur Foundation, "2008 MacArthur Fellows: Will Allen," Sep. 2008)
http://www.progressillinois.com
   (Progress Illinois, "A Growing Movement: Urban Farming in Chicago," Sep. 9, 2008)
http://www.urbanitebaltimore.com
   (Urbanite, "MacArthur Award Winner Will Allen on Raising Food—and Farmers—in the Inner City," Nov. 2008)

ADDRESS

Will Allen
Growing Power
5500 West Silver Spring Drive
Milwaukee, WI 53218

WORLD WIDE WEB SITES

http://www.growingpower.org

2005 © SPARC www.sparcmurals.org

Judy Baca 1946-

American Mural Artist, Educator, and Community Arts Pioneer

Creator of the Collaborative Murals *The Great Wall of Los Angeles* and *The World Wall: A Vision of the Future without Fear*

BIRTH

Judith Francisca Baca was born on September 20, 1946, in Los Angeles, California. She never knew her father, Valentino Marcel, who was a musician. She was raised by her mother, Ortencia, who worked in a tire factory. Baca has a half-brother, Gary, who was born in 1952, and a half-sister, Diane, who was born in 1957.

YOUTH

Baca grew up in a Spanish-speaking household in Watts, a predominantly Mexican-American neighborhood in south central Los Angeles. She lived with her mother, her grandmother Francisca, and her aunts Rita and Delia. While her mother worked to support the family, Baca was cared for mostly by her grandmother. Known as the neighborhood healer, Baca's grandmother practiced *curanderismo,* a form of Mexican folk medicine that combines traditional beliefs and herbal remedies to cure illness.

In a household of independent, self-sufficient women, Baca learned to form her own opinions at an early age. "The formative years, the most important years, were really good for me because, first of all, I didn't have any sense of the limits of what women could do," she recalled. "I did not have the appropriate role models of what girls were supposed to do or not do." Baca has said that she was very happy during these early years.

> "The formative years, the most important years, were really good for me because, first of all, I didn't have any sense of the limits of what women could do," Baca recalled. "I did not have the appropriate role models of what girls were supposed to do or not do."

In 1952, when Baca was six years old, her mother married Clarence Ferrari. Baca, her mother, and her new stepfather moved to Pacoima, a suburb of Los Angeles in the San Fernando Valley. Baca's whole world changed with that move. Mexican Americans were the minority in her new neighborhood, and her Italian stepfather did not allow Spanish to be spoken at home. Her grandmother and aunts stayed behind in the old neighborhood, and Baca missed them very much.

EDUCATION

Baca had a difficult time when she started school. She was not allowed to speak Spanish at school, even though she didn't understand very much English. Some of her teachers and classmates treated her unfairly because she was Mexican American. Baca struggled with her classes and worked hard to learn English quickly so that she could understand her textbooks and what was being said around her.

As Baca improved in English, her schoolwork became easier. She did well in every class, but her favorite was art. With the encouragement of her art teacher, she began to spend as much time as she could painting and drawing. In 1964, Baca graduated from Bishop Alemany High School in Mission Hills, California.

After high school, Baca attended California State University at Northridge, where she continued studying art. At that time, abstract modern art was very popular in art schools and galleries. Abstract art does not portray objects and people as they actually are. Instead, abstract artists use different colors and shapes to show how they imagine things to be, or to tell a story with pictures. Sometimes abstract art looks so unusual that people may not understand it at first. Abstract modern art is usually displayed in galleries, museums, or inside other buildings. Baca liked painting abstract art, but she also wanted to make art that was easy for people to understand and available for everyone to see.

Baca knew that she wanted to make art for the people in her life, like her grandmother, her aunts, and others in the neighbhorhood where she grew up. But they did not go to galleries to look at art. "I thought to myself, if I get my work into galleries, who will go there? People in my family had never been in a gallery in their entire lives. My neighbors never went to galleries. All the people I know didn't go to galleries.... And it didn't make sense to me at the time to put art behind some guarded wall." Baca decided that she would make art that was somehow connected to her Mexican-American background. She would combine the abstract artist's way of seeing the world with the bright colors and bold shapes that were traditionally found in Mexican folk art.

"I thought to myself, if I get my work into galleries, who will go there? People in my family had never been in a gallery in their entire lives. My neighbors never went to galleries. All the people I know didn't go to galleries.... And it didn't make sense to me at the time to put art behind some guarded wall."

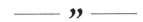

In 1969, Baca received a bachelor of arts (BA) degree in art from California State University at Northridge. She earned a master of arts (MA) degree in art education in 1979 from the same university.

CAREER HIGHLIGHTS

After more than 40 years as an artist, Baca is best known for her murals in public places. She has created murals in a wide variety of forms, including painting, tile mosaic, digital imaging, and collages incorporating

Baca has often involved the community in creating her art work, particularly young people. Here she is shown with the mural crew at The Great Wall of Los Angeles, 1983. © SPARC *www.sparcmurals.org*

such different materials as photographs, letters, and original artwork. Her murals cover a range of subjects, often reflecting her commitment to social justice and her heritage as a Chicana. These subjects have included the history of California, the journey of immigrants from Mexico to Colorado, civil rights, visions of world peace, and memorials to such renowned individuals as Dr. Martin Luther King Jr., Robert F. Kennedy, and Cesar Chavez.

Baca's work is founded on time-honored mural techniques established by generations of Mexican and Mexican-American artists, and many art experts see echoes of this artistic tradition in her murals. But she has also expanded this tradition, experts say, moving it a step forward. For example, she has developed new ways to design murals using computers and new methods of installing murals in public spaces so the artwork can be better preserved over time. As a result, Baca is considered a pioneer in the field of mural-making.

Becoming an Artist

Baca first began making murals in 1969. She had just graduated from California State University and found her first job teaching art at her former high school. She liked her job, but she found that different groups of students did not get along with each other very well. This was causing problems throughout the school. It was difficult for teachers to manage their classrooms, and students often fought outside of class.

Baca had an idea that she thought would help students learn to cooperate with each other. She decided to have a group of students work together to paint a mural on one of the school's walls. She explained to the group of students that they would have to figure out how to get along with each other and work together on the mural. Everyone wanted to participate in the mural project, so they learned to work with each other without fighting. Baca hoped that by helping the students work together on the mural, they might also be able to learn to cooperate with people in other areas of their lives. This was her first attempt at a cooperative art project, with many people working together to make art, and also her first attempt at a project involving young people. It was a success.

Baca's success in teaching at that high school was short-lived, however. Around the same time that she started teaching, she became involved in *El Movimiento* ("the movement"). In the mid-1960s and early 1970s, people who participated in *El Movimiento* worked for civil rights, peace, and an end to discrimination against Hispanic Americans. Baca took part in demonstrations and protests against the Vietnam War. The principal of the school where she taught believed that teachers should not take part in these protest marches. Baca and several other teachers were fired for their participation.

Working for the City of Los Angeles

At first Baca was worried that she would never find another teaching job because she had taken part in the controversial anti-war protests. However, she was soon hired by the city of Los Angeles to work in their Parks and Recreation Department. In her new job, Baca taught art for a summer program in the city's public parks. There she worked with people of all ages, in many different neighborhoods.

One neighborhood, known as Boyle Heights, had the most Mexican Americans as well as the highest number of gangs in the country at that time. Members of different gangs hung out in each of the parks where she worked, and there was gang graffiti everywhere. Baca knew that the graffiti marked the territory of each gang. The graffiti was a way for the gang members to feel like the neighborhood belonged to them, and that they belonged in that neighborhood. "You could read a wall and learn everything you needed to know about that community." One of her favorite graffiti markings was "I'd rather spend one day as a lion than a hundred years as a lamb."

As Baca traveled from one park to another teaching in the art program, she started to see the deep divisions within the community of Boyle Heights. She had begun getting to know many of the teeanagers who spent time in each of the parks where she worked. Baca saw that she had the freedom to go to any park in the neighborhood, but these teenagers did not. Each gang stayed in its own park or faced the consequences of fighting with a rival gang in another park.

> "It seemed to me that the only real answer if art was not to be an elitist practice was to bring it to the people, to paint in the places where people lived and worked."

Baca wanted to find a way to use art to bring the neighborhood together, instead of dividing the community the way the gang's graffiti did. She decided to create a mural in Boyle Heights. She wanted to use the mural as a positive way for people to feel that the neighborhood was theirs. To do this, the mural would be a cooperative art project, with many people working together on it.

Las Vistas Nuevas and *Mi Abuelita*

In the summer of 1970, Baca created her first mural team. She included 20 members of four different gangs and named the team *Las Vistas Nuevas* ("New Views"). The mural created by Las Vistas Nuevas would show images that would be familiar to the Mexican Americans who lived in the neighborhood. Baca wanted the mural to reflect the community's Mexican heritage. "I want to use public space to create a public voice for, and a public consciousness about people who are, in fact, the majority of the population but who are not represented in any visual way," she declared. In the process of making the mural, she hoped that team members would learn to share public spaces and respect each other, and, most importantly, that they could get along with people from different gangs. In this way, Baca hoped the team members would get a new view of themselves, their neighborhood, and their lives.

The first mural created by Las Vistas Nuevas was on the three walls of an outdoor stage in Hollenbeck Park. Titled *Mi Abuelita* ("My Grandmother"),

Mi Abuelita *was Baca's first collaborative mural, and the grandmother's outstretched arms made it a welcoming image in the community. Located in Hollenbeck Park band shell, the mural was developed with a youth team, Las Vistas Nuevas, from four neighborhoods in East Los Angeles. 20 ft. x 35 ft., acrylic on cement. © SPARC www.sparcmurals.org*

the mural's central image was a typical Mexican-American grandmother with her arms outstretched as if to give a hug. "This work recognized the primary position of the matriarch [female leader] in Mexican families," she observed. "It also marked the first step in the development of a unique collective process that employs art to mediate between rival gang members competing for public space and public identity."

Baca faced many challenges with this first mural. She had to help her team members learn to work together in spite of their differences. Every day, there were problems with gang members who were not on the mural team and didn't like what she was doing. They tried to interfere with the project by threatening team members and vandalizing the work site. The local police didn't like the idea of Baca encouraging rival gang membes to gather together because they thought it would increase gang violence. Also, she had started to work on the mural without permission from the city or the manager of Hollenbeck Park, which raised questions from her supervisor and other city officials.

In spite of all this, Baca was dedicated to completing the mural, so she handled problems as they arose. She posted lookouts who would signal the mural team if rival gang members were headed toward the work site. Another signal let the team know if police officers were approaching. One day, a city official came to Hollenbeck Park because he had been getting complaints about Baca's project. After seeing the progress that the team had made, and how well everyone was getting along with each other, he told Baca that she could finish the mural with the city's permission. "The city was amazed at the work I was doing," she stressed, "making murals with kids who scared directors out of neighborhood centers."

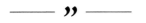

"This work [Mi Abuelita] *recognized the primary position of the matriarch [female leader] in Mexican families," Baca observed. "It also marked the first step in the development of a unique collective process that employs art to mediate between rival gang members competing for public space and public identity."*

Response to *Mi Abuelita*

When *Mi Abuelita* was completed, the community loved it. The mural brought the neighborhood together, and the grandmother figure with its outstretched arms became a symbol for unity. "Everybody related to it," Baca recalled. "People brought candles to that site. For 12 years people put flowers at the base of the grandmother image." During the rest of that summer, Las Vistas Nuevas completed a total of three murals in Boyle Heights.

After proving herself with the success of her independent mural project, Baca was offered a job in 1970 as the director of a new citywide mural program. She was put in charge of creating the program from the ground up, including choosing where murals would go, designing the murals, and supervising the mural painting teams. Team members were teenagers who had been in trouble with the police. Members of the original Las Vistas Nuevas team were hired to help run the multi-site program. The program included hundreds of young people representing many different ethnic and cultural backgrounds, and ultimately they painted more than 500 murals under Baca's direction.

While running the citywide mural program, Baca had her first problems with censorship. People in the communities where the murals were being

A view of The Great Wall of Los Angeles, *a 13 ft. x 2,400 ft. mural located in the Tujunga Wash, a flood control channel. The world's longest mural depicts a multi-cultural history of California from prehistoric times. This section of the wall shows the later panels depicting the 1950s. Acrylic on cast concrete.*
© SPARC www.sparcmurals.org

made wanted the murals to show all the parts of life in their neighborhood—both good and bad. The city government, however, did not want the murals to show anything controversial. For example, the city objected to part of one mural that showed people struggling with police. The city threatened to stop funding the mural program if Baca did not remove these images. She did not think that the city should censor public art created by residents of the community. "I really liked the idea that the work could not be owned by anyone," Baca explained. "So, therefore it wasn't going to be interesting to the rich or to the wealthy, and it didn't have to meet the caveats of art that museums would be interested in." Rather than give in to the city's demands, Baca founded the Social and Public Art Resource Center (SPARC) in 1976 to continue funding the creation of murals in public spaces.

The Great Wall of Los Angeles

SPARC began work on its first cooperative mural project in 1976. The U.S. Army Corps of Engineers hired Baca to help them improve the area around a San Fernando Valley flood control channel known as the Tujunga

Wash. This channel was basically a ditch that contained a large concrete retaining wall. The Army Corps of Engineers wanted to put a public park in the space, and they asked Baca to plan a mural for the wall.

The wall was 13.5 feet high and a half mile long—2,435 linear feet of concrete standing just below ground level. Baca's idea for the mural was to paint a history of the city of Los Angeles, but not the version found in history books. She wanted to show the events that were usually overlooked or forgotten and to include the stories of everyday people who lived and worked in Los Angeles as the city grew over time. "It was an excellent place to bring youth of varied ethnic backgrounds from all over the city to work on an alternate view of the history of the U.S. which included people of color who had been left out of American history books," she commented. The mural was to be titled *The Great Wall of Los Angeles*. According to Baca, the mural's defining metaphor would be the statement "It is a tattoo on the scar where the river once ran."

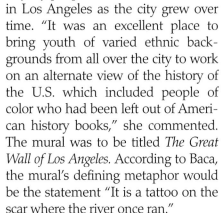

"Making a mural is like a big movie production," Baca said about creating **The Great Wall**, *which took seven summers to complete and is thought to be the world's longest mural. "It can involve 20 sets of scaffolding, four trucks, and food for 50 people."*

In her work on murals, Baca was inspired by the book *Los Tres Grandes (The Three Greats)*. This book was about three of the most influential Mexican muralists: Diego Rivera, David Alfaro Siqueiros, and José Clemente Orozco. These three artists had modernized the centuries-old Mexican tradition of mural painting by pioneering new techniques, ideas, and styles. In 1977, Baca traveled to Mexico to see their murals first-hand. Although none of the three famous muralists were still living at that time, she was able to work with some former students of Siqueiros. From them she learned about advanced mural painting methods and the materials that she ultimately applied to the large-scale outdoor project *The Great Wall.*

Baca decided that the design of *The Great Wall* mural should be a cooperative project. She interviewed people about their lives, family histories, ancestry, and stories they remembered hearing from their older relatives. She also consulted many other artists as well as history experts. Putting together everything that she learned from these conversations, Baca began creating the design for the mural. It would include many different scenes illustrating the development of Los Angeles, with panels depicting these scenes arranged chronologically along the wall. One section showed dinosaurs in a tar pit. Another section featured Spanish explorers arriving in their ships. There were images of Chinese workers building the railroad, Mexican farm workers in the fields, and other immigrants arriving in California with hope for a better life. Baca also illustrated such controversial events as the great Dust Bowl Journey, the Zoot Suit Riots of 1942, Japanese Americans being taken to internment camps during World War II, and the Freedom Bus Rides. Some of these sections of *The Great Wall* represented the first time the events had ever been acknowledged in such a public way.

Baca also decided that the painting of *The Great Wall* mural should be a cooperative project. Painting was done by groups of teenagers and adults of all ages and backgrounds. Some were scholars and artists, but many were simply community members. Some were paid workers, while others were volunteers. "Making a mural is like a big movie production," Baca said, "it can involve 20 sets of scaffolding, four trucks, and food for 50 people." In the end, 400 people contributed to the mural, which took seven summers to complete. *The Great Wall,* completed in 1984, is thought to be the world's longest mural. It has been called "the largest monument to interracial harmony in America" and a "landmark pictorial representation of the history of ethnic peoples of California from their origins to the 1950s." It stands as one of Baca's greatest accomplishments.

The World Wall

In the early 1980s, while still working on *The Great Wall,* Baca took a teaching position at the University of California at Irvine. In 1981, she developed the Muralist Training Workshop to teach other artists the techniques she had learned. Around this time, she was reminded of a comment from one of the young people who worked on *The Great Wall,* who said to her, "Wouldn't it be great if we could take this project all over the world?" Baca began to think about expanding the idea of *The Great Wall* mural to include a worldwide scope. She thought that if the concepts of cooperative mural making could be successful in Los Angeles communities, the same idea might be successful on a global scale.

In 1987, Baca began painting *The World Wall: A Vision of the Future Without Fear.* She envisioned this new mural as a far-reaching depiction of a world without violence. Baca believed that the first step toward world peace was to imagine it, and she wanted to involve artists from around the world in the creation of that vision. She also realized that in order to be seen by as many people as possible, in as many countries as possible, this new mural would have to be portable. She decided that the mural would be created in panels

Begun in 1990, The World Wall *is an international traveling mural installation consisting of numerous transportable panels with the theme "a vision of the future without fear." When the piece was shown in Mexico City, the panels were separated and mounted as individual artworks. Eight panels totaling 10 ft. x 240 ft., acrylic on canvas. © SPARC www.sparcmurals.org*

that could be moved around to different places. The piece is also adaptable, since the individual panels can be shown as one continuous work, in traditional mural form, or as separate works, with the panels arranged in a variety of ways. *The World Wall* is an attempt to push the state of arts in muralism so that the mural creates its own architecture," she explained. "It makes its own space and can be assembled by any people anywhere."

After several years of planning, and with the contributions of many different artists, *The World Wall* had its debut in Finland in 1990. As the mural traveled on to be shown in other countries, the artist team in each country would add their panel to the display. Currently, *The World Wall* includes panels from Finland, Russia, Israel/Palestine, Mexico, and Canada, along with four panels from Baca and her Los Angeles team. *The World Wall* will grow to 14 panels, and perhaps more.

Meanwhile, in 1988 the mayor of Los Angeles wanted Baca to create a new mural program for the city. Once again, she agreed to lead a mural program for Los Angeles. The program, known as Great Walls Unlimited:

Neighborhood Pride, was given the goal of painting a mural in almost every ethnic neighborhood of Los Angeles. To meet this goal, Baca and SPARC trained hundreds of artists and young people. Over the course of many years, the Neighborhood Pride program painted 105 murals throughout the city, commissioned works from 95 established or emerging artists, and employed over 1,800 young apprentices.

Creating the Future of Murals

In addition to creating countless murals in public spaces, Baca has devoted her career to teaching others how to make murals. While working at SPARC, she has taught at several universities in California. Baca began her academic career at the University of California-Irvine, where she worked as a professor in the Studio Arts department from 1981 to 1994. From 1994 to 1996 she was a professor at California State University-Monterey Bay, where she co-founded the Visual and Public Art Institute

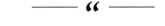

"I am a Mexican mural painter in the true sense, but I took it to the next level," Baca declared. *"To keep an art form living, it has to grow and change."*

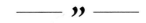

Program. In 1996 she moved to the University of California-Los Angeles (UCLA), where she has taken on multiple roles. While serving as a professor in UCLA's Cesar Chavez Center for Interdisciplinary Instruction in Chicana and Chicano Studies, she has also served on the Center's board and has taught in UCLA's World Arts and Cultures department.

In addition, Baca created the UCLA/SPARC Cesar Chavez Digital Mural Lab. The lab is a research, production, and teaching facility that uses modern technology in community-based art programs. The lab offers opportunities for those in low-income communities to have access to state-of-the-art technology. It brings local youth and their families together with students at UCLA to create community-based public art. At the same time, it brings UCLA students together with Baca so they can learn how to use computer technology to create murals.

Through work in this lab, Baca has pioneered several new techiques in mural-making. She developed one technique that uses digital imaging in murals, combining traditional mural-painting techniques with computer-generated imagery. "I draw hundreds and hundreds of sketches, look at things from thousands of different perspectives to make sure that I'm preparing a site well," she said. "With the computer I am able to see the work ... from a variety of perspectives and directions, thus eliminating the need for hundreds of sketches.... I could also eliminate hours and hours of work." Baca also developed a technique for creating murals on thin sheets of aluminum that can be attached to the interior or exterior walls of buildings. These murals can then be easily removed for cleaning or restoration, or saved in the event that the buildings are torn down. "I am a Mexican mural painter in the true sense, but I took it to the next level," she declared. "To keep an art form living, it has to grow and change."

"I struggle not to be lost from my culture because I think it is the very spirit of how I work," Baca affirmed. "My work is informed by my connection. There's force in the connection. It is the base from which the work flows."

One example of the way that Baca combines these two new techniques in mural-making is her work titled *La Memoria de Nuestra Tierra (Our Land Has Memory)*, which she created for the Denver International Airport in Colorado. This mural shows the history of the land that is now Colorado and the people who lived there. The project was a very personal one for Baca, because her grandparents fled Mexico during the Mexican revolution and traveled to Colorado to escape the war. Baca wanted to use this mural "not only to tell the forgotten stories of people who, like birds or water, traveled back and forth across the land freely, before there was a line that distinguished which side you were from, but to speak to our shared human condition as temporary residents of the earth.... The making of this work was an excavation of a remembering of their histories."

Completed in 2000, *La Memoria de Nuestra Tierra* is 10 feet high and 50 feet long. The mural combines painting with digital images and historical documents and is printed on a sheet of bronze-colored aluminum. "With the use of computer technology I have incorporated these images and documents into the mural," Baca explained. "The landscape imagery was hand painted at a small scale and then scanned into the computer at a very high resolution for inclusion into the mural ... a meticulously hand painted landscape with historic photographs in a seamless blend." It has been called "a breakthrough in digital murals."

In 2008, Baca's work in murals took on a new form. For the *Cesar Chavez Monument Arch of Dignity, Equality, and Justice,* she designed a 25-foot arch with individual digital mural panels. The monument is located at San Jose

For the 2008 Cesar Chavez Monument Arch of Dignity, Equality, and Justice, *shown here, Baca designed a 25-foot arch with individual digital mural panels. This monument at San Jose State University consists of murals of farm workers, Cesar Chavez, Mahatma Gandhi, and Dolores Huerta. The monument was designed by Baca and the UCLA/SPARC Cesar Chavez Digital Mural Lab.*
© SPARC www.sparcmurals.org

State University in San Jose, California. It consists of farm workers featured in two murals painted and printed digitally, a portrait of Cesar Chavez painted and then produced in full color Venetian tile, along with portraits of Mahatma Gandhi and Dolores Huerta. The monument, which was designed by Baca and the UCLA/SPARC Cesar Chavez Digital Mural Lab, commemorates Chavez through his ideals and beliefs, carried out in his actions to improve the conditions of the farm workers, which inspired so many to join his efforts to achieve social justice. A key element to the monument is to teach members of the next generation how to choose to live a life in the center of their values and beliefs, as Cesar Chavez did.

Saving the Murals of LA

In recent years, a movement has been underway to save the murals of Los Angeles—those created by Baca, as well as those created by many other artists. Over the years, many murals have been damaged by sunlight, water, and exposure to the elements, while some have been ravaged by vandalism. To address this problem, SPARC began a new campaign called

Save LA Murals (SLAM) to raise funds, to act as advocates for this public art, and to organize people to take action.

One mural affected in this way is *The Great Wall of Los Angeles,* which has been extensively damaged. The 35th anniversary of the project's start is approaching in 2011, and Baca and SPARC are now working to restore the mural to its original condition. They are also adding new sections illustrating the decades after the 1950s, where the original mural ended. Unlike most art restoration, which involves experienced experts, the restoration of *The Great Wall* is being done in the same way that the work was originally created—by *Great Wall* alumni, youth, and community members.

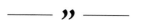

> "*I have had a very blessed life,*" *Baca said.* "*I've gotten to dream dreams and make them be. Who gets to do that? Pretty cool.*"

Baca has argued that one reason for the damage to the existing murals is that new murals haven't been created recently. Young people don't have any personal involvement with the murals, so they don't develop any respect for them. "Murals have become history, and not current life," she reasoned. "Young people began to mark on the murals for the first time. We need to reeducate the young people about the importance of the murals. A generation has not worked on them—their brothers, their sisters, their friends, have not been on a mural. Painting is really just one step for making a dream real. You imagine it, you visualize it, you create it, and then it becomes more tangible, and it becomes important to the people because they can see it on a daily basis. And then put it where the people live, put it where they work. It becomes embedded in the consciousness, and it becomes part of the fabric of a community. That's why the murals are important—and that's why they're important to be preserved."

For Baca, creating art shouldn't be limited to artists. She believes that everyone can create art and that art can be a tool for social change and self-transformation. "Break the mold! Have the biggest vision you can! If you can't dream it, it cannot occur." Reflecting on her own work as an artist, Baca said, "I have had a very blessed life. I've gotten to dream dreams and make them be. Who gets to do that? Pretty cool."

MARRIAGE AND FAMILY

Baca married when she was 19 years old and still in college. The marriage ended in divorce six years later. She continues to live in Venice, California.

SELECTED WORKS

Mi Abuelita, 1970
Medusa Head, 1973
Las Tres Marias, 1976
History of Highland Park, 1977
Hitting the Wall: Women in the Marathon, 1984
The Great Wall of Los Angeles, 1984
Guadalupe Mural Project, 1990
The World Wall: A Vision of the Future without Fear, 1990 (ongoing)
Danzas Indigenas, 1994
Raspados Mojados, 1994
Local 11, 1998
La Memoria de Nuestra Tierra: Colorado, 2000
Durango Mural Project: Recollections, 2002
Digital Tile Murals on the Venice Boardwalk, 2003
Migration of the Golden People, 2003
Cesar Chavez Monument Plaza, 2008

SELECTED HONORS AND AWARDS

Educator of the Year (National Association of Art Educators): 1988
Rockefeller Fellowship Award (UCLA Chicano Studies Research Center):
   1991
Lifetime Achievement Award (National Hispanic Magazine): 1997
Influential Woman Artist Award (Women's Caucus for Art): 1998
Master Artist and Senior Scholar (Harvard University): 1998
Creative Vision Award (Liberty Hill Foundation): 2001
Hispanic Heritage Award (National Hispanic Heritage Foundation): 2001,
   for Educator of the Year
Montgomery Fellowship (Dartmouth College): 2002
John Simon Guggenheim Fellowship): 2003
Named One of 100 Most Influential Hispanics (Hispanic Business Maga-
   zine): 2005
Self-Help Graphics Master Artist Series: 2008
Champions of Change Award (Escuela Tlatelolco Cenro de Estudios): 2009
Elizabeth "Betita" Martinez Activist Scholar Award (InnerCity Struggle):
   2009
Judy Chicago's Through the Flower Awards: 2009, for contribution to femi-
   nist art movement
White House Briefing on Arts, Community, Social Justice, and National
   Recovery: 2009

FURTHER READING

Books

Fernandez, Mayra. *Judy Baca: Artist,* 1994 (young adult)
Isenberg, Barbara. *State of the Arts: California Artists Talk about Their Work,* 2000
Liu, Eric. *Guiding Lights: The People Who Lead Us Toward Our Purpose in Life,* 2004
Olmstead, Mary. *Judy Baca,* 2005 (young adult)

Periodicals

Hispanic Magazine, May 1991, p.17
Los Angeles Daily News, Oct. 21, 2007, p.N1
Los Angeles Times, Aug. 10, 1993, p.8; Dec. 1, 1997, p.3; Aug. 19, 2001; Jan. 6, 2009
New York Times, Sep. 19, 1997, p.A18; Apr. 28, 1998; May 26, 2002, sec. 2, p.29
People, May 24, 2004, p.98
Wall Street Journal, Sep. 29, 2000

Online Articles

http://www.pbs.org/americanfamily/mural.html
    (PBS.org, "The Art of the Mural," 2004)
http://www.aaa.si.edu/collections/oralhistories/transcripts/baca86.htm
    (Smithsonian Institution, "Judith Baca Interviews," Aug. 5, 1986)
http://latino.si.edu/virtualgallery/ojos/bios/bios_Baca.htm
    (Smithsonian Institution, "Judith F. Baca," 2004)

ADDRESS

Judy Baca
SPARC
685 Venice Blvd.
Venice, CA 90291

WORLD WIDE WEB SITES

http://www.judybaca.com
http://www.sparcmurals.org
http://www.savelamurals.org

Joe Biden 1942-

American Political Leader and Six-Term U.S. Senator
Vice President of the United States

BIRTH

Joseph Robinette Biden Jr. was born on November 20, 1942, in
Scranton, Pennsylvania. His father, Joseph Robinette Biden,
worked as a boiler cleaner and car salesman and later owned
his own car dealership. His mother, Jean (Finnegan) Biden,
was a homemaker. He has two younger brothers, James and
Francis, and one younger sister, Valerie.

YOUTH

Biden grew up in a working-class neighborhood in Scranton, an industrial city located in the northeastern corner of Pennsylvania. The Biden home was modest, and the family never had much money. Biden recalled that he even used to put cardboard in his shoes to cover up holes in the soles. But his parents created a loving and supportive home for all their children, and Biden has many fond childhood memories.

Biden says that his mother taught him many valuable lessons about life as he was growing up. She taught him to believe in himself and in the importance of family. In his autobiography, *Promises to Keep,* he recalled that she often said, "Remember, Joey, you're a Biden. Nobody is better than you. You're not better than anybody else, but *nobody* is any better than you."

Biden also noted, however, that his mother believed deeply that all people deserved respect and consideration. "The one thing my mother could not stand was meanness," he said. "She doesn't have a mean bone in her body, and she couldn't stand meanness in anybody else. She once shipped my brother Jim off with instructions to bloody the nose of a kid who was picking on smaller kids, and she gave him a dollar when he'd done it."

>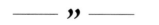
>
> "The one thing my mother could not stand was meanness," Biden recalled. "She doesn't have a mean bone in her body, and she couldn't stand meanness in anybody else. She once shipped my brother Jim off with instructions to bloody the nose of a kid who was picking on smaller kids, and she gave him a dollar when he'd done it."

Biden's father also played a major role in shaping the children's moral character and outlook. "There was no daylight between my mom's philosophy of life and my dad's," Biden wrote in his autobiography. "She was just more vocal about it…. Dad was the keeper of the rules at the table—our manners were to be impeccable—and he liked to nudge the conversation toward big issues like morality, justice, and equality."

Joe Biden Sr. also provided a shining example to his children of how to handle disappointments and setbacks in life with grit and grace. During the 1930s and early 1940s he had been a successful businessman who raced cars, flew in private planes, and wore expensive business suits. His wealth vanished during the late 1940s, though, due to a thieving business partner. This turn of events was difficult for Biden Sr. to absorb, especially because he had a growing family to support. But he refused to wallow in bitterness or despair about the downturn in his fortunes. Instead, he dusted himself off and quietly worked long hours as a used car salesman to support his family. "He never, ever gave up, and he never complained," Biden wrote of his father. "He had no time for self-pity. He didn't judge a man by how many times he got knocked down but by how fast he got up."

Overcoming a Speech Problem

The general happiness that marked Biden's childhood was marred by one problem that tormented him on a daily basis. He struggled with a stutter, a speech disorder in which normal sentence flow is disrupted by repeat-

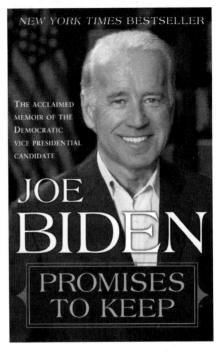

In his memoir, Biden includes stories about his early life and career, showing the guiding principles that helped him overcome the many setbacks he faced along the way.

ed expressions of the same sounds, syllables, and words. People who experience these speech "roadblocks" are no less intelligent than people who can converse without any problems. But they often become the target of teasing and taunting in childhood.

Stuttering problems vary greatly from person to person, and Biden's disorder was not as severe as some cases. "When I was at home with my brothers and sister, hanging out with my neighborhood friends, or shooting the bull on the ball field, I was fine," he recalled in *Promises to Keep*. "But when I got thrown into a new situation or a new school, had to read in front of the class, or wanted to ask out a girl, I just couldn't do it…. Even today I can remember the dread, the shame, the absolute rage, as vividly as the day it was happening."

Sports provided a welcome escape for Biden. "As much as I lacked confidence in my ability to communicate verbally, I always had confidence in my athletic ability," he recalled in his autobiography. "Sports was as natural to me as speaking was unnatural. And sports turned out to be my ticket to acceptance—and more. I wasn't easily intimidated in a game, so even when I stuttered, I was always the kid who said, 'Give me the ball.' Who's going to take the last shot? 'Give me the ball.' We need a touchdown now. 'Give me the ball.' I'd be eight years old, usually the smallest guy on the field, but I wanted the ball. And they gave it to me."

——— " ———

Biden had a problem with stuttering when he was young. "When I was at home with my brothers and sister, hanging out with my neighborhood friends, or shooting the bull on the ball field, I was fine," he recalled. "But when I got thrown into a new situation or a new school, had to read in front of the class, or wanted to ask out a girl, I just couldn't do it.... Even today I can remember the dread, the shame, the absolute rage, as vividly as the day it was happening."

——— " ———

In 1953 the Biden family moved from Scranton to Claymont, Delaware, where his father continued to work as a car salesman. It was in Claymont that young Joe Biden finally conquered his stutter. He practiced public speaking for hours in front of a mirror at home and gradually learned to "beat" the disorder. By the time he graduated from high school, he was an accomplished and confident public speaker. Biden even gave the commencement address at his high school graduation in 1961.

EDUCATION

Biden attended Roman Catholic parochial schools in Scranton and Claymont for his elementary education. He attended high school at Archmere Academy, a private Catholic prep school in Claymont, on a special work-study program that helped his family with the tuition. He was a solid B student in high school who was popular with his classmates. "In almost any group I was the leader," he recalled. "I was class representative my sophomore year and class president my junior and senior years. I might have been student body president, but Father Diny [who headed Archmere] wouldn't let me run— too many demerits."

After graduating, Biden enrolled at the University of Delaware in the fall of 1961. He played safety on the football team and loved the social whirl on campus. He later admitted that he was not very disciplined about his studies, but college roommates recall that he was never in danger of flunking out. "He had a talent for getting it done when it had to get done," recalled one college roommate. Another friend from his college days added that "Joe was the kind of guy who could read someone else's notes and do better on the exam than the guy who made the notes."

During his junior year at Delaware, Biden went to the Bahamas for spring break. During his stay he met Neilia Hunter, an attractive college student from Syracuse University who was also on spring break. The two of them quickly struck up a close relationship, and Biden later admitted that in his case it was "love at first sight." Their love affair became so intense that he quit the football team to spend more time with her. And after earning his Bachelor of Arts (BA) degree from Delaware in 1965, he decided to attend law school in Syracuse, New York, where Hunter had secured a teaching job.

Biden entered Syracuse University College of Law in the fall of 1965, and one year later he married Hunter. He was not a particularly good student at Syracuse—he graduated 76th in a class of 85—but he excelled in the courses that really engaged his interest. In addition, he discovered at Syracuse that he possessed an actual talent for speaking before audiences. "What had terrified me in grade school and high school was turning out to be my strength," he recalled in his autobiography. "I found out I liked speaking in public.... I fell in love with the idea of being able to sway a jury—and being able to see it happen right before my eyes." In 1968 Biden earned his Juris Doctor or Doctor of Law (JD) degree from Syracuse. He and Neilia then promptly moved back to Delaware, where he had received a job offer from a prominent legal firm.

FIRST JOBS

Biden had worked a wide range of jobs as a youngster, from lifeguarding to landscaping. He knew after leaving Syracuse that he was entering the "real" world; the careless approach that he had taken to college classwork would get him fired in a law office. As a result, Biden had little trouble adjusting to the long hours required of a young attorney, and he passed the Delaware bar exam on his first try in 1968. But he disliked the conservative political orientation of the big firm, and in 1970 he established his own small legal firm in downtown Wilmington.

Biden developed a reputation as a strong and sympathetic defender of accused criminals and poor people trapped in expensive legal cases. But in

Biden is shown with his two sons, Beau and Hunter, and his wife, Neilia, while campaigning for a seat in the U.S. Senate. This shot was taken in 1972, just a few months before his wife and young daughter were killed in a terrible car accident. Shown here on the left are governor-elect Sherman Tribbitt and his wife, Jeanne Tribbitt.

the early 1970s he became even better known around Wilmington as a member of the New Castle County Council. Biden won a seat on the council in 1970 as a Democrat, even though the district was mostly Republican. He spent the next two years developing a reputation as "the guy who took on the builders and the big corporations," in his own words. Biden supported new job-creating businesses, but he also challenged projects that he thought were damaging to the environment or the welfare of the wider community.

CAREER HIGHLIGHTS

Biden's performance as a county councilman captured the attention of Democratic Party leaders across Delaware. Taking note of his energy, good humor, and liberal political beliefs, they saw him as a rising young star in Delaware politics. They were horrified, though, when the 29-year-old Biden announced his intention to seek the U.S. Senate seat held by J.

Caleb Boggs. Party leaders thought he was crazy to challenge Boggs, who had been a popular governor in Delaware in the 1950s, then gone on to win two terms as a U.S. senator.

Biden defied their predictions and pulled out a narrow victory in the November 1972 election. One factor in his surprise win was a strong set of positions in support of environmental protection, civil rights, labor unions, and new health care and mass transit programs. But Biden never would have succeeded without the help of his family. In addition to his wife Neilia, who took care of their three young children and encouraged and counseled him every day, Biden got help from his sister, Valerie, who served as his campaign manager. Her husband volunteered to be the campaign's budget director, and Jean Biden organized dozens of small "coffee hour" speaking engagements for her son all across Delaware.

> *"The moment exceeded all my romantic youthful imaginings," Biden said about election night. "I was a United States senator-elect at age 30. Our family was together under one splendid roof. The doors were just beginning to swing open on the rest of our lives. Neilia and I had done this amazing thing together, and there was so much more we would do. Neither of us was sure exactly what the rest of our lives would bring, but we couldn't wait to see."*

Biden's victory made him the youngest senator in U.S. history to win by popular election. Political observers noted that, when he took his oath of office in January 1973, he would become the fifth-youngest senator in the history of the U.S. Congress. Years later, he recalled savoring his victory on election night with his wife in front of the big crackling fireplace at their home. "The moment exceeded all my romantic youthful imaginings," he later wrote. "I was a United States senator-elect at age 30. Our family was together under one splendid roof. The doors were just beginning to swing open on the rest of our lives. Neilia and I had done this amazing thing together, and there was so much more we would do. Neither of us was sure exactly what the rest of our lives would bring, but we couldn't wait to see."

Family Tragedy Strikes

A few weeks later, Biden's life was shattered by a tragic accident. His wife, Neilia, and their one-year-old daughter, Naomi, were killed in a car accident while out shopping for a Christmas tree. Their two young sons—Beau and Hunter—were also in the car, and they were critically injured. When Biden rushed to the hospital and heard the horrible news, he recalled that "I could not speak, only felt this hollow core grow in my chest, like I was going to be sucked inside a black hole."

Biden spent the next several weeks in his sons' hospital room as they slowly recovered from their injuries. He initially planned on giving up the senate seat he had just won so that he could devote all his time to his sons. But his sister and brother-in-law agreed to move to Wilmington to help him care for his boys. In addition, Senate Majority Leader Mike Mansfield offered him a number of prestigious senate committee assignments if he would agree to take the job on a six-month trial basis. Biden agreed after a great deal of soul-searching, and in January 1973 he took part in a swearing-in ceremony held in his sons' hospital room.

When Biden took office, every other U.S. senator lived in Washington DC or across the Potomac River in northern Virginia. Biden, however, knew that it would be easier for his sons to recover emotionally from the loss of their mother and little sister if they did not have to adjust to a new living environment. He decided to commute to work from Wilmington by Amtrak train. The 80-minute one-way trip made life a little more hectic, but he never regretted the decision. "Family has always been the beginning, the middle, and the end with me," he explained.

During his first term as senator, Biden did not go out of his way to make friends in Washington. He did his job, then took the train home while other Congressional leaders went out to expensive restaurants and fancy social events. "I think he was far more interested in his children than the social whirl," recalled Senator Patrick J. Leahy.

Biden decided to finish out his six-year term out of a sense of obligation to Delaware voters, but he doubted that he was going to seek re-election. Then, in 1976, he became involved in a romantic relationship with Jill Jacobs, a teacher in the Wilmington area. When they married one year later, Biden knew that Jill would be there for his sons if he decided to continue his political career in Washington. He decided to run for a second term in 1978, and he easily won re-election.

Biden campaigning in Chicago for the Democratic nomination for president, 1988. Biden, left, is shown with Chicago Mayor Harold Washington, Illinois Sen. Frank Demuzio, civil rights leader Jesse Jackson, and U.S. Sen. Paul Simon.

"A Happy Warrior"

During the late 1970s and 1980s Biden became a well-known figure in the U.S. Senate. Throughout this period he served as the top Democrat (either as chairman or ranking minority member) on the Senate Judiciary Committee, one of the most visible and important committees in Congress. He also compiled a voting record that won high praise from liberal groups and voters.

At the same time, though, Biden exhibited a strong independent streak. On the issue of abortion, for example, he believed that women should have the right to choose whether to end their pregnancies without interference from government authorities. But despite angry condemnation from liberal groups, he steadfastly opposed the use of federal money for any abortion services. "It's the only consistent position [to have] intellectually," he insisted. "If you say government should be out [of the process], government should be out."

Within Congress, most of Biden's fellow senators viewed him as a cheerful and friendly fellow who nonetheless enjoyed a spirited argument. "He's a happy warrior," said one colleague. "He loves the whole thing, but he'll punch you out [in a debate]." Another older senator who often worked with Biden freely acknowledged that "Joe gets worked up," but argued that his sharp tongue reflected his convictions. "Some people think he gets too candid sometimes, but that's a mark of his generation. Better his short fuse than no fuse at all." Biden was not universally admired, though. Some rivals and observers grumbled that he was a showboat and a know-it-all.

In early 1987 Biden decided to make a run at the biggest political job in the world: president of the United States. After formally announcing his candidacy for the 1988 Democratic presidential nomination on June 9, 1987, he began dividing his time between Washington DC and the campaign trail. Biden's bid for the presidency lasted less than four months, though. In September his campaign was rocked by accusations from journalists and political opponents that he had plagiarized speeches delivered by British politician Neil Kinnock. Biden insisted that he usually credited Kinnock in his speeches, but that he forgot to do so at a single campaign event. The controversy refused to go away, however, and he eventually realized that his presidential candidacy was doomed. Even after ending his campaign, though, Biden remained squarely in the public spotlight. Upon returning to Washington, he played a major role in defeating the nomination of conservative lawyer Robert Bork for the U.S. Supreme Court in the fall of 1987.

Rebuilding His Career

In early 1988 Biden's life took a frightening turn for the worse. He suffered a ruptured brain aneurysm—an abnormal swelling in a blood vessel that can cause fatal levels of internal bleeding when it bursts. After two surgeries and seven months of recovery, Biden was finally able to return to the Senate, but the experience changed him forever. Vowing to put the controversies of 1987 behind him, he rededicated himself to his work in the U.S. Senate. "I understood that a single moment of failure—even one so public and wounding as the end of my presidential campaign—could not determine my epitaph," he wrote in his autobiography. "I had faith in the ultimate fairness and reason of the American people, and I had faith that I could rebuild my reputation."

Over the next several years, Biden became one of the Senate's most authoritative and influential voices on foreign policy issues. He was recognized as an expert on the Middle East and Asia, and he played a significant role in convincing President Bill Clinton to use military air strikes to stop horrible human rights violations in Eastern Europe in 1999.

During this same period, Biden enjoyed the greatest legislative triumph of his senate career: the passage of the Violence Against Women Act

Biden worked tirelessly on behalf of the Violence against Women Act of 1994, which funded programs that helped women who had been victims of rape or abuse. He is shown here at a news conference with Sen. Barbara Boxer (at the podium). Behind them, from left, are Rep. Constance Morello, Rep, Pat Shroeder (behind Boxer), and Rep. Carolyn Maloney (far right).

(VAWA) of 1994. Before this law was passed, most communities had no shelters to house victims of abuse or rape, and police departments were frequently unfriendly—or at least poorly equipped—to handle reports from women who had been battered or raped. Biden was outraged by the situation, and he wrote and sponsored a bill that would fund the construction of shelters, educate police about violence against women, and enable cities to hire counselors and prosecutors dedicated to the issue. Other senators tried to kill VAWA because of its price tag, but Biden refused to give in. "You can sponsor a bill, but if you just sponsor a bill and let it sit there, that's nothing," said one activist who worked with Biden. "He shepherded [VAWA]. He made sure it happened. He assigned staff to it, gave them carte blanche to do what they needed, they spent days and nights on it."

Biden's tireless efforts helped get VAWA through both houses of Congress, and President Clinton signed the bill into law in 1994. It proved so successful in reducing violence against women—and so popular with voters—that

Biden with Barack Obama at the 2008 Democratic National Convention, where they were nominated as their party's candidates for president and vice president.

it was reauthorized in both 2000 and 2006 with support from Republicans and Democrats alike. "If I were to choose the single most important event leading to broad-based awareness and change regarding domestic and sexual violence against women," said one domestic violence activist, "it would be Senator Biden's Violence Against Women Act of 1994."

Becoming Obama's Running Mate

By the time Republican George W. Bush became president in 2001, Biden's career seemed almost fully recovered. He routinely cruised to victory at election time, claiming 60 percent or more of the vote in both 1990 and 1996. In addition, he regularly represented his party on national television shows like "Meet the Press" and "Face the Nation." This comeback did not surprise Alan Hoffman, who served as Biden's chief of staff for several years. "He has a deep conviction and pride in the work he does, so failure doesn't always bother him," said Hoffman. "He always bounces back. Always. It doesn't even surprise me anymore." As the decade wore on, he emerged as one of the most visible critics of the Bush administration. He expressed profound regret for supporting Bush's invasion of Iraq in 2003, and he challenged the president on a wide range of domestic and foreign policy issues.

In January 2007 Biden announced his intention to launch another campaign for the White House. But when the list of Democratic presidential candidates rapidly expanded to include high-profile politicians like Senator Hillary Clinton, former vice presidential candidate John Edwards, and Senator Barack Obama, Biden's candidacy was ignored by the national media. After several impressive debate performances failed to ignite interest in his campaign, Biden realized that he should drop out. He left the race in January 2008, then watched with great interest as Obama narrowly beat out Clinton for the Democratic nomination.

During the summer of 2008, Biden's name repeatedly came up in discussions about possible vice presidential candidates for Obama. Many political observers thought that Biden's foreign policy experience and ability to attract working-class voters would help Obama deal with accusations that he was weak in those areas. One day, Biden received a call from Obama, who asked him whether he would be interested in the vice presidency. If so, he would have to undergo "vetting"—an intense investigation of all aspects of his private and professional life to check for unknown scandals. Biden recalled the conversation vivid-

"I started my career fighting for civil rights," Biden remarked, "[and to make history] with a guy who has such incredible talent and who is also a breakthrough figure in multiple ways—I genuinely find that exciting. It's a new America."

ly: "Obama called to ask me whether or not I would be willing to be vetted—and he was very specific, he said, 'I'm not fooling around, it's down to three or fewer people, I'm not asking you to jump into a mix of ten people—would you be willing?' And I said, 'I have to think about it.'"

Biden's cautious response came from two concerns. First, he already had a position that gave him great satisfaction and influence. "It wasn't self-evident to me that being vice president would be a better job—you know what I mean?" he later told the *New Yorker*. Second, Biden wanted to make sure that he and Obama shared the same vision for the country's future, and that the vice president would play a meaningful role in an Obama administration. When further conversations with Obama reassured Biden, he agreed to be considered for the slot.

A few weeks later, Obama formally asked Biden to be his vice presidential running mate. Biden accepted, and on August 23, 2008, Obama an-

Inauguration Day—Surrounded by his family, Biden is sworn in as vice president by Supreme Court Justice John Paul Stevens on January 20, 2009.

nounced his selection to the world. Democrats reacted positively to the pick, and even some Republicans praised Obama's decision. "Biden is good-natured, serious, and truly qualified," stated Ed Rogers, who served as a member of the White House staff in the presidential administrations of Republicans Ronald Reagan and George H.W. Bush. "Everyone who cares about good government and serious politics can imagine him as president."

Other political observers were more critical of Biden's selection. The most vocal criticism came from supporters of Republican presidential candidate John McCain. They charged that Biden's background did not compensate for Obama's "inexperience." In addition, they ridiculed the Delaware senator for some of his past verbal blunders. But as election day approached, the Obama camp seemed happy with their choice. "Joe Biden's strength is he speaks his mind, and every once in a while it may not come out the right way—a speed bump," said Obama advisor David Axelrod. "But those things were minor, and frankly did not hurt us. When you take the few times when he may have said something that would make you kind of scratch your head and weigh it against the good he did us, it isn't even a close contest."

Becoming Vice President of the United States

Throughout the fall of 2008, there was non-stop campaigning by the two tickets—Barack Obama and Joe Biden for the Democrats and John McCain and Sarah Palin for the Republicans. Biden proved to be an energetic and enthusiastic campaigner for the Democratic ticket. He delivered a strong performance in the lone vice-presidential debate against Republican vice presidential candidate Sarah Palin, and he appeared at rallies all across the country to generate support for Obama's candidacy. Time and time again, he argued that Obama's policies provided the best antidote for the many domestic and international problems facing the nation.

On election day, November 4, 2008, the American people made their choice. The Obama-Biden ticket easily defeated the McCain-Palin ticket. Obama and Biden claimed 53 percent of the popular vote (7 percent more than the Republicans) and 365 electoral votes (compared to 173 for McCain-Palin). These election results were truly historic, for they made Obama the first African-American president-elect in U.S. history.

Afterward, Biden expressed delight with the decisive victory, as well as gratitude to be part of such a historic event. "I started my career fighting for civil rights," he remarked, "[and to make history] with a guy who has such incredible talent and who is also a breakthrough figure in multiple ways—I genuinely find that exciting. It's a new America."

> ———— " ————
>
> *"I'm genuinely optimistic [for the future]," Biden said in early 2009. "It's going to be rough until we climb of out of this.... But I think we've got a ladder long enough, and I think when we climb out of this hole ... [we will] climb onto a platform that's clearer, sturdier, better, more competitive for America, and put us in a position where we're able to do in the 21st century what we did in the 20th century. I really, genuinely believe that."*
>
> ———— " ————

Biden observed that the Obama administration will face difficult challenges, from resolving unpopular wars in Iraq and Afghanistan to reviving a sick American economy. "This is the worst of times to come into office," he acknowledged. "The responsibilities, the burdens, the crises exceed anything—and I said it during the campaign and I believe it even more now—

that any president has faced since Franklin Roosevelt.... But the flip side of that is, if you're ever going to do this job, this is the time to do it. If you're a surgeon, do you want to do a tonsillectomy or a heart transplant?"

Despite these challenges, Biden's reputation as "a happy warrior" remains intact. "I'm genuinely optimistic [for the future]," he said in early 2009. "It's going to be rough until we climb of out of this.... But I think we've got a ladder long enough, and I think when we climb out of this hole ... [we will] climb onto a platform that's clearer, sturdier, better, more competitive for America, and put us in a position where we're able to do in the 21st century what we did in the 20th century. I really, genuinely believe that."

MARRIAGE AND FAMILY

Biden married Neilia Walker in 1966. They had three children—Joseph "Beau," Robert "Hunter," and Naomi. Neilia and Naomi were killed in a car accident in December 1972. Beau grew up to become the state attorney general for Delaware, and in October 2008 he was deployed to Iraq as a captain in the Delaware National Guard. Hunter is an attorney.

Biden was a single father for five years, until he married educator Jill Jacobs on June 17, 1977. They had one daughter together, Ashley, who is a social worker.

During Biden's years as vice president, he and his wife will live in the official vice presidential residence in Washington DC. This 19th-century Victorian-style mansion with 33 rooms is located on the grounds of the U.S. Naval Observatory, next to the British embassy. This move brought Biden's 36-year-streak of Amtrak commuting to an end. But the Bidens intend to keep their home in Wilmington and use it as their retirement home.

HOBBIES AND OTHER INTERESTS

Biden enjoys reading about history and many other subjects. He served for many years as an adjunct professor at the Widener University School of Law in Wilmington, where he taught a seminar on constitutional law.

WRITINGS

Promises to Keep, 2007

SELECTED HONORS AND AWARDS

Congressional Leadership Award (National Center for Missing and Exploited Children): 2004

George Arents Pioneer Medal (Syracuse University): 2005
Best of Congress Award (*Working Mother* magazine): 2008

FURTHER READING

Books

Biden, Joe. *Promises to Keep,* 2007

Periodicals

Christian Science Monitor, Aug. 28, 2007, p.15
CQ Weekly, Dec. 30, 2000, p.98
Current Biography Yearbook, 1987
Esquire, Feb. 2009, p.78
Los Angeles Times, Aug. 27, 2008, p.A10
National Journal, July 16, 2005, p.2281
New York Times, Sep. 1, 2008, p.A14; Oct. 2, 2008, p.A1; Oct. 24, 2008,
    p.A17; Nov. 3, 2008, p.A18; Nov. 26, 2008, p. A14; Feb. 8, 2009, p.A6; Feb.
    20, 2009, p.A15
New Yorker, Mar. 21, 2005, p.32; Oct. 20, 2008, p.48
Newsweek, Oct. 13, 2008, p.46
Time, Nov. 10, 2008, p.44
U.S. News & World Report, Sep. 21, 1987, p.24; Nov. 17, 2008, p.26
USA Today, Aug. 25, 2008, p.A1; Aug. 28, 2008, p.A4
Washington Post, Aug. 24, 2008, p.A1; Aug. 25, 2008, p.A17
Washingtonian, Dec. 1985
Weekly Standard, Jan. 5-Jan. 12, 2009, p.14

Online Articles

http://abcnews.go.com/WN/WhoIs/story?id=3770445&page=1
    (ABC World News, "Get to Know Joe Biden," Dec. 13, 2007)
http://www.nytimes.com/2007/12/14/us/politics/14biden.html
    (New York Times, "Biden Campaigning with Ease after Hardships," Dec.
    14, 2007)
http://topics.nytimes.com/top/reference/timestopics/people/b/joseph_r_jr_
    biden/index.html
    (New York Times, "Times Topics," collected articles, various dates)
http://topics.time.com/joe-biden/0,30939,,00.html
    (Time, "Time Topics," collected articles, various dates)
http://projects.washingtonpost.com/2008-presidential-candidates/joe-biden
    (Washington Post, "Joe Biden," no date)

ADDRESS

Vice President Joe Biden
The White House
1600 Pennsylvania Avenue NW
Washington, DC 20500

WORLD WIDE WEB SITES

http://www.barackobama.com
http://www.whitehouse.gov

Lupe Fiasco 1982-

American Rap Artist and Entrepreneur
Grammy-Award Winning Creator of the Hit Records
Food & Liquor and *The Cool*
Founder of the Companies 1st & 15th (FNF) and
Righteous Kung-Fu

BIRTH

Lupe Fiasco was born Wasalu Muhammad Jaco on February 17, 1982, in Chicago, Illinois. His mother, Shirley, worked as a gourmet chef. His father, Gregory, worked as an operating plant engineer and also owned Army Surplus stores and a martial arts school. Fiasco has nine brothers and sisters, of which six are half brothers and sisters.

YOUTH

Fiasco, called Lu as a child, grew up on the west side of Chicago, Illinois. His family lived in an apartment in Chicago's Madison Terrace housing project. The neighborhood was rough, but Fiasco's parents worked hard to help their children thrive. "I grew up in the 'hood around prostitutes, drug dealers, killers, and gangbangers," he explained. "On the doorknob outside of our apartment, there was blood from some guy who got shot; but inside, there was National Geographic magazines and encyclopedias and a little library bookshelf situation. And we didn't have cable, so we didn't have the luxury of having our brains washed by MTV. We watched public television—cooking shows and stuff like that."

> **"I did martial arts." Fiasco recalled." If I had to fight, I could defend myself. But it also taught me how to see when a fight is coming and how to defuse it. I learned how to think. That's the most important thing my mother and father taught us."**

Fiasco's parents exposed their children to a wide range of experiences, including the culture of Chicago's many different ethnic groups. He credits these early adventures as a major influence on his development as an artist. "My father was a real prolific African drummer, and can play anything from the djiembes [African drums] to the bagpipes. My mom is a gourmet chef that has traveled the world. We were always around different cultures. It is because of these artistic experiences there are no limitations to what I talk about on my records."

Fiasco's father had also been a member of the Black Panthers civil rights activist group and a former Army Green Beret. His father was also a martial arts master. Under his direction, Fiasco began practicing martial arts when he was only three years old. "My father told me to respect weapons," he recalled. "I learned to respect them so much that I never wanted one. I did martial arts. If I had to fight, I could defend myself. But it also taught me how to see when a fight is coming and how to defuse it. I learned how to think. That's the most important thing my mother and father taught us." By the time he was ten years old, Fiasco had already earned four black belts in martial arts and two in samurai swords.

Fiasco loves skateboarding, which was the subject of one of his first hit songs, "Kick Push."

When Fiasco was five years old, his parents divorced. After that, Fiasco lived with his mother, but his father continued to be a strong presence in his life. "After school, my father would come get us and take us out into the world—one day, we're listening to [rap group] N.W.A., the next day,

———— " ————

Fiasco and his family were devout Sunni Muslims. "We would go to different mosques around the city," he recalled. "Each mosque would be in a different community, so it would be a different ethnic group. It would be Pakistanis, it would be Indians, it would be Palestinians, or it would be Africans.... I got to see a lot of different people.... It's like we were almost traveling the world.... I got exposed to a lot of different cultures."

———— " ————

we're listening to [Indian sitar player] Ravi Shankar, the next day, he's teaching us how to shoot an AK-47, the next day, we're at karate class, the next day, we're in Chinatown.... We experienced everything with my father because the things he was into were so vast." With this type of experience, Fiasco began developing his musical tastes even before he started school, becoming interested in jazz and classical music. By the time he was six years old, he loved listening to the music of Beethoven and Tchaikovsky, playing the same records over and over.

For Fiasco and his family members, these cultural explorations extended to their religious practice as devout Sunni Muslims. "We would go to different mosques around the city," he recalled. "Each mosque would be in a different community, so it would be a different ethnic group. It would be Pakistanis, it would be Indians, it would be Palestinians, or it would be Africans.... So I was always all over the city in different neighborhoods. I got to see a lot of different people.... It's like we were almost traveling the world.... I got exposed to a lot of different cultures."

Fiasco's mother has described him as "a great spirited child. Smart, a bit complex; he kind of was a loner, he didn't hang with a lot of people.... He always had the glasses, always had a book bag over his shoulder and some kind of a writing tablet. He loved to skateboard, too. You could hear those little raggedy wheels … ka-kunk-ka-kunk-ka-kunk, all night long." Fiasco loved reading comics and any other kind of books. His childhood favorites were Dr. Seuss, the Berenstain Bears, the science fiction novels of Jules Verne and George Orwell, and the books of Mark Twain.

EDUCATION

When Fiasco was in the sixth grade, he went to live with his father in the south Chicago suburb of Harvey, Illinois, and attended school there. Science was his favorite subject, and he especially liked chemistry. He thought of pursuing a scientific career but abandoned that goal because his math skills were not good enough for advanced study in the sciences. In high school, Fiasco discovered a love of the theater, and he ran the lights and sound for most of the school's theatrical productions. He joined the chess club and was also a member of the school's Knowledge Bowl Decathlon Team. Fiasco graduated from Thornton Township High School in Harvey, Illinois.

CAREER HIGHLIGHTS

Becoming a Rapper

Fiasco first began rapping in eighth grade because he wanted to find a way to express himself through music. "I come from a literary background, and I loved to tell stories. I remember freestyling stories, not in rhyme, by just coming up with things when I was a kid on the bus. But I couldn't play an instrument, so I decided to take my storytelling mind and to apply it to rap, which seemed like a natural thing. So I practiced a lot and really tried to apply the techniques I'd learned from poetry—which, of course, is the predecessor of rap."

At first, Fiasco tried out stage names like Little Lu and Lu tha Underdog. But by the time he was in high school, his friends were calling him Lupe. Then he chose the name Fiasco from a track called "Firm Fiasco" by hip-hop supergroup The Firm. Although some people tried to talk him out of the name, he was committed to it. "I simply liked the way the word looked. You know how rappers always have names like MC Terrorist—like they're 'terrorizing' other rappers? I knew fiasco meant a great disaster or something like that, but I didn't realize that the person named Fiasco would be the disaster, and that you should be calling other MCs fiascos—not yourself. I was moving real fast at the time, and it kind of humbled me in a sense. It taught me like, 'Yo, stop rushing, or you're going to have some fiascos.' So I just kept it. It's like a scar, I guess, a reminder to not overthink or overrun anything ever again."

By the time he was 17 years old, Fiasco was thinking seriously about a career as a rapper. Although his parents didn't like the idea of their son pursuing a career as a hip-hop performer, his father allowed him to set up a recording and mixing studio in the basement. Fiasco scoured Chicago's flea markets and secondhand stores, where he bought the necessary equipment: an old mixing board and record player, a stack of old vinyl records, and mic stands. Working with a group of friends, Fiasco rigged the studio and began making demo tapes and remixes of songs by other artists.

Soon Fiasco had formed a rap group called Da Pak. Copying the style of California gangsta rappers like Spice 1 and Ice Cube, Da Pak began performing wherever they could. In 2000, when Fiasco was 19 years old, Da Pak signed a contract with Epic Records. But the success of the group was short-lived, and Da Pak disbanded after releasing their first single. "We had a song out about cocaine, guns, and women," he said, "and I would go to a record store and look at it and think, 'What are you doing?' I felt like a hypocrite. I was acting like this rapper who would never be judged, and I had to destroy that guy. Because what Lupe Fiasco says on this microphone is going to come back to Wasalu Jaco. When the music cuts off, you have to go home and live with what you say."

In turning away from the violent images of gangsta rap, Fiasco found that he was more attracted to the lyricism of rappers like Nas and Jay-Z. Around this time, his mother gave him some recordings of 1960s poetry performance groups like the Watts Prophets, who were among the first to use spoken word with music in a format that would later evolve into rap.

> "We had a song out about cocaine, guns, and women," Fiasco said, "and I would go to a record store and look at it and think, 'What are you doing?' I felt like a hypocrite. I was acting like this rapper who would never be judged, and I had to destroy that guy. Because what Lupe Fiasco says on this microphone is going to come back to Wasalu Jaco. When the music cuts off, you have to go home and live with what you say."

The First Big Break

Fiasco was inspired and determined to build his career as a rapper. By 2001, he founded a music production company called 1st & 15th (also known as FNF), named after the traditional twice-monthly paycheck dates. He signed a recording contract with Arista records, but the deal fell through. However, the Arista deal wasn't a complete failure because it allowed Fiasco to meet Jay-Z, who was then the president of Def Jam Records. Jay-Z called Fiasco a "breath of fresh air" and said Fiasco reminded him of himself early in his career. In 2004, Jay-Z helped Fiasco get a new contract with Atlantic Records. Fiasco then began recording the tracks that would eventually become his first album.

While he worked on his new music, Fiasco released his critically acclaimed mixtape series *Fahrenheit 1/15* over the Internet. As word spread, his remix-

Fiasco's first album, Food & Liquor, *was nominated for four Grammy Awards and won one award.*

es were downloaded by people all over the world, quickly resulting in a global fanbase. His remix "Muhammad Walks," based on Kanye West's "Jesus Walks," became popular with Muslims all over the world.

Fiasco's big break came when his track "Conflict Diamonds," a remix of Kanye West's "Diamonds from Sierra Leone," caught West's attention. West was so impressed with the remix that he invited Fiasco to perform on his upcoming single "Touch the Sky." The success of Fiasco's contribution to "Touch the Sky" resulted in the early release of his first official solo single. Entitled "Kick Push," this skateboard-themed song was inspired by Fiasco's own childhood hobby and soon became a hit. "It's a skateboarding song. I used to skateboard when I was younger. I was really into it. I never really knew that skateboarding was so deep as a culture. It's just as deep as hip-hop." "Kick Push" was nominated for two 2007 Grammy Awards.

Food & Liquor

Fiasco's first full-length album, *Food & Liquor,* was released in 2006. The album's artwork shows him surrounded by a collection of various items, including a ninja doll, a Nintendo game console, and a copy of the Muslim holy book, the Koran (also spelled Qur'an). He explained the image on the cover like this. "All of that is out of my book bag. It's the stuff I carry around every day." The album's title also has a significant meaning for Fiasco. "The title reflects on me being Muslim and being from the streets. In Chicago, instead of having bodegas like in New York, the majority of the corner stores are called 'Food and Liquors.' The store is where everything is at, whether it be the wine-o hanging by the store, or us as kids going back and forth to the store to buy something. The 'Food' is the good part and the 'Liquors' is the bad part. I try to balance out both parts of me…. Food to me represents growth and progression. You eat food and you get strength. You need it to live. Liquor is not a necessity; it is a want. It destroys you. It breaks you down. I can see why it's prohibited in Islam…. I've always felt like liquor represents the bad, and food represents the good, and everyone is made up of a little of both."

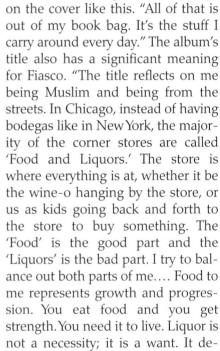

> "*Without dipping his toes into violent imagery, wanton obscenity, or other hip-hop clichés," wrote one* **Rolling Stone** *reviewer, "Fiasco reflects on the personal and the political, and reminds fans of everything hip-hop can be. It's full of surprising, creative moments."*

Food & Liquor received rave reviews, with some music critics even calling Fiasco "the savior of the genre." Fiasco was praised for his storytelling talent and his ability to present mature subject matter grounded in his Muslim faith. A *Rolling Stone* reviewer said, "Without dipping his toes into violent imagery, wanton obscenity, or other hip-hop clichés, Fiasco reflects on the personal and the political, and reminds fans of everything hip-hop can be. It's full of surprising, creative moments." His raps were called complex, thought-provoking, and playful, and the beats were praised as inventive. An *Interview* magazine critic said, "The album straddles hip-hop and rock, with songs that segue from funky blaxploitation grooves into grunge, cabaret, and swirling cinematic string arrangements."

Food & Liquor was widely considered one of the best hip-hop records of the year and received a total of four Grammy nominations. In 2007, *Food & Liquor* was nominated for Best Rap Album, and "Kick Push" won two nominations, for Best Rap Song and Best Rap Solo Performance. The following year, "Daydreamin'" was nominated for and won the Grammy Award for Best Urban/Alternative Performance. The album also received four BET Hip Hop Award nominations. It appeared on several Billboard music charts, ranking No. 8 on the Billboard 200 and taking the No. 2 spot on Billboard's Top R&B/Hip-Hop Albums chart.

The Cool

Fiasco's second album, *The Cool,* was released in 2007. The album's title is taken from a track on *Food & Liquor,* and several tracks on *The Cool* expand on the story presented in the original song. Here Fiasco introduces three distinct characters: Michael Young History, representing "My Cool Young History"; The Game, representing the damaging influences of greed, vice, and hustling; and The Streets, representing temptation and corruption. Fiasco explained the story told in these songs. "It's about how The Cool starts off as this little boy, he grows up without a father, he's raised by The Game, falls in love with The Streets, goes on to be this big-time hustler, gets killed, and comes back to life…. Digs his way out of his own grave, and goes back to his old neighborhood and gets robbed by these two kids, ironically with the same gun he was shot with."

The Cool was described as a dark examination of life's pleasures, but Fiasco was careful not to glamorize any aspect of the story. He believes that what people think is "cool" will ultimately dominate every choice they make, positive or negative. "I always put myself as a storyteller first. I talk about the same concepts as Young Jeezy, but I deglamorize it and put it on a cinematic level that leaves it open to interpretation. So in essence, the story is of all of us. The Cool, The Streets, and The Game—those characters represent all of us…. In high school I was a nerd, and I haven't changed. Nerds, those with or without glasses, are the coolest people on this planet. The stuff that they do and the things that they talk about and the outlook they have on life…. This is the theory that runs my existence as a rapper…. If you want to effect change in society, you have to make it cool to be uncool; you gotta make it hip to be square. Because it is the things that have been made hip that destroy us and that we will be blamed for…. I want the cool things to become uncool, and the world will be less destructive."

The Cool also includes some tracks that are not directly related to this story. In "Superstar," Fiasco raps about becoming famous and dealing with too much attention, including the lyrics "A fresh, cool young Lu, trying to cash his microphone check, 2, 1, 2, wanna believe my own hype, but it's too untrue, the world brought me to my knees." In "Hello Goodbye," he compares recording artists to slaves being owned by a music industry that promotes "the faith that being a slave is so great."

One *Rolling Stone* reviewer said that in *The Cool*, "bleak raps clash with the smoothed-out vibe of the music, maybe even more than they're supposed to, and some of the tracks fall short.... Fiasco speaks in the voice of the ultimate con man—a drug dealer, a slave trader, a politician, and a rapper.... It's a scary sound." However, other critics found plenty to praise in Fiasco's second album, including its soft, jazzy R&B feel and the tough lyrics that attacked hip-hop's materialistic culture. *Entertainment Weekly* credited Fiasco's mass appeal to his "versatile beats, melodic pop hooks, and articulate lyrics."

The Cool proved to be a big hit with fans and with critics. It received four Grammy nominations: the album was nominated for Best Rap Album; "Paris, Tokyo" was nominated for Best Rap Solo Performance; and "Superstar" (with Matthew Santos) was nominated for Best Rap Song and Best Rap/Sung Collaboration. The album also appeared on several Billboard music charts, ranking No. 14 on the Billboard 200 and No. 4 on the Top

R&B/Hip-Hop Albums. The track "Superstar" appeared on Billboard's Pop 100, Hot Rap Tracks, and Top 40 Mainstream.

Next Projects

After the release of *The Cool,* Fiasco formed a hip-hop supergroup known as CRS (Child Rebel Soldiers) with Kanye West and Pharrell. CRS released the single "Us Placers," and all three artists appeared on West's Glow in the Dark tour in 2008. In 2009, Fiasco was honored as one of the USA Network's Character Approved award winners. The award included a $10,000 donation to a charity chosen by each winner. Fiasco gave his donation to Action Against Hunger, an international network committed to helping malnourished children and families, saying, "I love to feed people, especially those in need." Fiasco was also nominated for a 2009 Urban Music Award, for Best Hip Hop Act.

"In high school I was a nerd, and I haven't changed," Fiasco declared. "Nerds, those with or without glasses, are the coolest people on this planet. The stuff that they do and the things that they talk about and the outlook they have on life.... This is the theory that runs my existence as a rapper."

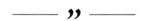

Fiasco plans to release at least three more albums before retiring as a recording artist. When creating new music, he prefers to focus on quality over quantity. Fiasco described his musical style as "'simple complexity.' I'm a big jazz fan. You might have the same three instruments but the beats, the rhythms, and everything they're doing is really, really complex. So I always take that approach when I make rap records." His Muslim faith also influences the subject matter included in his raps. "[Islam] affects my music as far as the stuff I don't talk about. I don't degrade women in my records. I try not to use profanity in my records or put anything negative in my records. I always try to put a positive message or solution in my records," Fiasco pointed out. "What you put out into the world comes back to you. You actually change the world with what you do. I want to put some good in the world."

HOME AND FAMILY

Fiasco considers Chicago to be his full-time home, although he has no permanent place to live there. "I'm kind of ... just living out of a suitcase.

Fiasco brings a lot of intensity to all his live performances.

I'm so busy.... I'm kind of a drifter. No place to really call home. I'd like to live in Paris. I'd like to see what Paris is talking about."

HOBBIES AND OTHER INTERESTS

When he is not rapping, Fiasco says he is usually writing. He would like to someday finish the novel he has been working on for years. "A lot of the stuff I want to say musically, it has a limit. You can't compress and process certain things into 16 bars, or a song. It needs to be in a book, or it needs to be in a dissertation, or a speech, or a movie."

Fiasco collects Japanese toys and robots, is fascinated by quantum mechanics and chaos theory, and enjoys reading the works of German philosopher Friedrich Nietzsche. He enjoys listening to all kinds of music, especially jazz. His favorite jazz recording is Robert Glasper's jazz piano album *G&B.* His favorite song is "Somebody to Love" by Queen, and he says that there are several Queen albums that he can sing word for word.

Fiasco also devotes much of his time to his various business ventures. In 2005, he founded Righteous Kung-Fu, a company that designs fashions, sneakers, toys, video games, comic books, and graphics for album covers and skateboard decks. He has endorsement contracts with Reebok and has designed logos for some Reebok shoes, including the "OG." Fiasco has sponsored a skateboard team and also has endorsements with skateboard outfitter DGK.

As a devout practicing Muslim, Fiasco does not drink alcohol, smoke, use drugs, or go to clubs or bars. He also doesn't skateboard any more, having given it up after a 2007 street-skating accident that he says might have killed him if he hadn't been wearing a helmet.

RECORDINGS

Food & Liquor, 2006
The Cool, 2007

HONORS AND AWARDS

AOL Music Award: 2006, Breaker Artist
Artist to Watch (*Rolling Stone*): 2006
MTV2 Freshest MC (MTV): 2006
Breakout Artist of the Year (*GQ*): 2007
Grammy Award: 2008, Best Urban/Alternative Performance, for "Daydreamin'"
Character Approved Award (USA Network): 2009

FURTHER READING

Periodicals

Billboard, July 15, 2002, p.24; Jan. 6, 2007, p.40; Dec. 1, 2007, p.30
Ebony, Dec. 2006, p.152
Entertainment Weekly, Oct. 27, 2006, p.72; Jan. 18, 2008, p.56
Interview, Mar. 2006, p.200
New York Times, May 15, 2008, p.1
Rolling Stone, Sep. 21, 2006, p.22

Online Articles

http://www.chicagomag.com/Chicago-Magazine/August-2007/Word-Star/
    (Chicago Mag, "Word Star," Aug. 2007)
http://www.mtv.com/music/artists
    (MTV, "Lupe Fiasco," undated)
http://www.rollingstone.com/artists/lupefiasco
    (Rolling Stone, "Lupe Fiasco Biography," undated)
http://soundslam.com
    (Soundslam, "Hip to Be Square," undated)

http://www.vibe.com/news/online_exclusives/2006/08/lupe_fiasco_weirder
_than_your_average/
(Vibe, "Lupe Fiasco: Weirder Than Your Average," Aug. 18, 2006)

ADDRESS

Lupe Fiasco
Atlantic Records
1290 Avenue of the Americas, 28th Floor
New York, NY 10104

WORLD WIDE WEB SITES

http://www.lupefiasco.com
http://www.atlanticrecords.com/lupefiasco/bio
http://www.usanetwork.com/characterapproved/honorees/fiasco
http://www.actionagainsthunger.org

James Harrison 1978-

American Professional Football Player with the
Pittsburgh Steelers
NFL Most Valuable Defensive Player in 2008

BIRTH

James Harrison Jr. was born on May 4, 1978, in Akron, Ohio.
His father, James Sr., worked as a chemical truck driver. His
mother, Mildred, was the primary caregiver for James and his
13 siblings.

YOUTH AND EDUCATION

Harrison was the youngest child in his large family, and his brothers and sisters picked on him sometimes. But his mother was a strict disciplinarian who made sure that things never got too out of hand. "The only person allowed to raise their voice at home was Mildred," she said about herself. She also worked hard to make sure that her youngest son never felt ignored or forgotten. To the contrary, Harrison grew up knowing that coming home late or other forms of misbehavior would result in stern punishment.

> *When Harrison was young, his mother didn't want him to play football. "I didn't want my son getting hurt running around on that field." But he and his best friend, David Walker, finally convinced her to let him give it a try. "I had to go and help convince his mom to let him sign up," remembered Walker. "We went together and begged her."*

Harrison loved football from an early age. His favorite National Football League (NFL) team was the Cleveland Browns, who played their home games only about 40 miles away from his hometown of Akron. He admits that he even used to cry when the Browns lost big playoff games. Harrison's own football career began over the objections of his mother, who recalled that "I didn't want my son getting hurt running around on that field." But he and his best friend from childhood, David Walker, finally convinced her to let him give it a try. "I had to go and help convince his mom to let him sign up," remembered Walker. "We went together and begged her."

From his earliest days of youth football, Harrison displayed uncommon strength and fearlessness on the field. He excelled at both linebacker and running back. By the time he entered high school, area coaches agreed that he was one of the most promising young players in Akron. Harrison attended two Akron-area high schools (Archbishop Hoban and Buchtel) as a freshman before ending up at Coventry High School in suburban Akron. He spent his last three years of high school at Coventry, from which he graduated in 1998.

Harrison was one of the best players in Coventry's history. His strength, speed, and intensity made him such a fearsome linebacker that college football scouts regularly sat in the stands to watch him play. His immaturity, though, nearly derailed his high school career at several different points.

Harrison (#16) at Kent State, making the tackle.

Harrison paid little attention to his grades or college entrance tests, and by his senior year he had become a disruptive presence on the football team. Early in his senior season, the Coventry staff suspended him for two games for challenging an assistant coach to a fight. Soon after his return to the lineup, he received a one-game suspension for making obscene gestures at opposing fans who were allegedly taunting him with racial insults. Harrison then found himself in court for firing a BB gun in the school locker room. He pleaded guilty to a minor charge and was able to return to school to finish out his senior year. But the incident—combined with his earlier suspensions—scared off major college football programs like Ohio State, Notre Dame, and Nebraska, which had shown interest in him earlier in the year.

CAREER HIGHLIGHTS

NCAA—Kent State Golden Flashes

When Harrison failed to obtain the football scholarship that he thought was coming his way, he decided to attend nearby Kent State University in Kent, Ohio. His parents agreed to pay for his freshman year. They hoped that if he made a strong showing in the classroom and on the football field, the school would take note and give him an athletic scholarship for his remaining years of school.

The football coaches for the Kent State Golden Flashes were happy to have such a talented athlete on their squad, but Harrison's poor study habits remained a big problem. He posted such terrible grades in his first semester that his mother nearly pulled him out of school once and for all. "When I got the first report card," she recalled, "I went up there with my brother and said, 'Get all his stuff and put it in the van. We're going home. I'm not paying for this.'" An alarmed Harrison was finally able to convince her to give him another chance. As he watched his mother drive away, though, he knew that he had to improve his grades.

> **Harrison's grades were so bad that his mother nearly pulled him out of college. "When I got the first report card," she recalled, "I went up there with my brother and said, 'Get all his stuff and put it in the van. We're going home. I'm not paying for this.'"**

The Kent State coaching staff helped Harrison by arranging extra tutoring help. In addition, they began demanding more accountability and effort from him on the practice field. "The guy [Harrison] was playing behind wasn't even close to as good as he was," recalled Dean Pees, who served as head coach during Harrison's years at Kent State. "He knew it. I knew it. He also knew I wasn't going to change. I wasn't going to play him until he gave me what he had."

Harrison buckled down in all phases of school. He raised his grades to become a 3.0 student, and he treated practice more seriously. At the start of his senior season, he was even selected as a team captain. As the 2001 season progressed, Harrison took his game to a new level of excellence, earning first team All Mid-American Conference honors at linebacker. His ferocious play helped lift Kent State to its first winning season in 14 years. Harrison left Kent State in the spring of 2002 a few credits shy of earning a bachelor's degree in general studies.

NFL—Pittsburgh Steelers

Despite Harrison's breakout senior season at Kent State, no NFL team claimed him in the 2002 draft. Pro scouts appreciated his competitive nature and tackling abilities. But they worried that he was too short (about six feet tall) to play linebacker in the NFL, yet too light (about 240 pounds) to be successful on the defensive line.

Harrison felt intense disappointment at going undrafted. A few teams, though, did approach him with offers to attend their upcoming training camps as a free agent (a player who is not under a long-term contract with a team). After weighing his options, Harrison decided to bid for a spot on the roster of the Pittsburgh Steelers, one of the most successful and respected franchises in the NFL.

Harrison spent the next year and a half trying to make the Steelers' roster. He showed flashes of tremendous potential, but Head Coach Bill Cowher and the rest of the Pittsburgh coaching staff cut him from the roster on three different occasions. Harrison suggested that he had trouble convincing the team that NFL linebackers could come in all shapes and sizes. "People said I was too short, too slow, couldn't do this or that," he recalled.

Teammates from that time period, however, indicate that the staff grew tired of Harrison's stubborn nature and his difficulties mastering defensive coordinator Dick LeBeau's complex schemes. "He was a knucklehead that didn't know the plays," said fellow linebacker James Farrior. "We'd be in practice, in training camp, and he might not know what he was doing so he'd just stop and throw his hands up and tell [the coaches] to get him out of there. We thought the guy was crazy."

Getting cut for a fourth time almost convinced Harrison to give up on the NFL. "I didn't want to be that guy who [keeps trying] to get in for three or four years and then it never happens," he explained. "I felt like I would have given it an honest two years, it didn't work, so it just wasn't meant to be. I would have found a regular job."

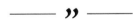

After Harrison was cut for the third time in February 2004, the Baltimore Ravens picked him up. They promptly shipped him off to Germany to play for the Rhein Fire in NFL Europe, a "developmental" league for promising young players and coaches. Harrison disliked living and playing in Germany, however, and in June 2004 Baltimore cut him loose.

Getting One Last Chance

Harrison returned to Akron after being let go by the Ravens. He was not sure what to do with his life at this point. He loved football, but he later admitted that getting cut for a fourth time almost convinced him to give up on the NFL. "I didn't want to be that guy who [keeps trying] to get in for

Harrison hurdles over San Diego Chargers' LaDanian Tomlinson while making a 25-yard interception, San Diego, 2005.

three or four years and then it never happens," he explained. "I felt like I would have given it an honest two years, it didn't work, so it just wasn't meant to be. I would have found a regular job."

Harrison briefly thought about becoming a veterinarian. He then decided to follow in his father's footsteps and seek a commercial driver's license.

But at that point he received an unexpected telephone call from the Steelers. The team informed him that one of its veteran linebackers, Clark Haggans, had injured his hand in a freak weightlifting accident. The Steelers asked Harrison if he wanted to try to make the team one more time. He accepted the offer and headed off for training camp.

When Harrison arrived at camp, he signaled his determination to make the most of this final chance at an NFL career. Unlike other teammates who relaxed in front of the television after a grueling day of practice, Harrison spent hours each night studying his playbook. He also adopted a different attitude on the practice field. "The way I took coaching, the way I talked to coaches ... that was all different," he said. "I had to change all of that because it was basically the last hurrah."

Coaches and teammates alike took note of Harrison's improved attitude. He made the Steelers roster for the opening of the 2004 season, and as the season progressed he became one of the top players on Pittsburgh's special teams, handling punts and kickoffs. On November 5, 2004, he made his first NFL start at linebacker when one of Pittsburgh's regular starters had to serve a one-game suspension. Harrison had five solo tackles, including a quarterback sack, and played well for all four quarters. "From that time on," recalled Le Beau, "we thought we had a chance of having a really special player."

By the end of the 2004 regular season, Harrison had earned a measure of job security with the Steelers. "He's developed into quite a football player," explained Coach Cowher. "He's matured tremendously from two years ago when he came here. He's taken a very professional approach. He prepares. He's an integral part of our special teams and I think he's going to be a pretty good linebacker in this league." The Steelers, meanwhile, won 15 out of 16 regular season games and looked poised to claim the fifth Super Bowl championship in the team's history. Harrison and his teammates were tripped up, though, in the AFC Conference Championship by the eventual Super Bowl champion New England Patriots by a score of 41-27.

Earning Rewards through Patience and Hard Work

Harrison spent the next two seasons in Pittsburgh as a valuable but mostly anonymous role player. He excelled on special teams and in occasional linebacker duty throughout the 2005 campaign, which turned into a special one for the Steelers. The team clinched a playoff berth with an 11-win, 5-loss regular season, then ripped off three straight victories in the playoffs to claim a spot in Super Bowl XL (40). When Pittsburgh defeated the Seat-

*Harrison sacks Ryan Fitzpatrick (#11) of the Cincinnati Bengals early in
the 2008 season, with the Steelers on their way to a Super Bowl and
Harrison on his way to Defensive Player of the Year.*

tle Seahawks in the Super Bowl by a 21-10 score, Harrison earned his first
Super Bowl ring.

The following year was a big disappointment for the Steelers. The team
struggled to an 8-8 record due to injuries and bad breaks, and Cowher retired at the end of the season. Harrison, though, remained confident that

the future remained bright for him in Pittsburgh. He respected the team's new head coach, Mike Tomlin, and at the end of the 2006 season the Steelers signed Harrison to a four-year, $6.5 million contract. Harrison knew that the generous contract reflected the team's strong belief that he was ready to become a starting linebacker.

This opportunity came in the 2007 season, when longtime starting linebacker Joey Porter left Pittsburgh to play for the Miami Dolphins. Harrison was placed in Porter's slot as a full-time starter, and he quickly proved that the Steelers had made the right choice. By the time the season was over, Harrison ranked second on the team in tackles (86) and first in quarterback sacks (8.5), and he had been elected to his first Pro Bowl. Moreover, he was credited with almost singlehandedly winning a Monday Night Football game against the Ravens in early November. Harrison racked up 3.5 quarterback sacks, forced three fumbles, and intercepted a pass before the night was through.

The Steelers posted a 10-6 record in 2007, which was good enough to get the team back in the playoffs. Pittsburgh lost in the first round, but NFL analysts predicted that the tough Steelers defense would make them a force to be reckoned with in 2008. And the Steelers coaches agreed that Harrison had become an important part of that squad. "To me, the story on James Harrison is a guy who never gave up on himself," said Le Beau. "[He] continued to work through the rejections, through the adversity, all the disappointments."

> "
>
> *"To me, the story on James Harrison is a guy who never gave up on himself," said defensive coordinator Dick LeBeau. "[He] continued to work through the rejections, through the adversity, all the disappointments."*
>
> "

A Dominant Force

Harrison was excited about the Steelers' prospects for the 2008 season. Before training camp even began, though, he faced renewed questions about his maturity and temperament. In March 2008 Harrison was charged with simple assault and criminal mischief for allegedly slapping his girlfriend, Beth Tibbott. The charges were eventually dropped by Tibbott after Harrison took responsibility for the incident and agreed to attend anger-management classes.

Once the 2008 season began, Harrison put the controversy behind him and concentrated on football. By mid-season, NFL experts and opponents were referring to him as a one-man wrecking crew. Opposing quarterbacks and running backs described him as a dominant force, and Harrison's teammates were quick to agree. "He demands a lot of attention," said Farrior. "And when you've got a guy like that dominating and making every play, it just opens the door up for everybody else." By the end of the season, Harrison and his defensive teammates were known around the league as the main reason for the Steelers' 12-4 record. The Pittsburgh defense allowed the fewest yards and fewest points in the entire NFL.

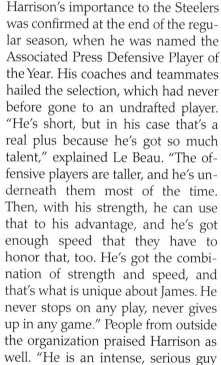

> *Harrison was excited leading up to Super Bowl XLIII. "It means a little bit more to me [this time] because I am a starter instead of playing just on special teams," he said, comparing his experiences in 2009 with those in 2006. "I have matured. I handle situations a lot differently now than I would back then.... I have learned the game and taken time to study the game."*

Harrison's importance to the Steelers was confirmed at the end of the regular season, when he was named the Associated Press Defensive Player of the Year. His coaches and teammates hailed the selection, which had never before gone to an undrafted player. "He's short, but in his case that's a real plus because he's got so much talent," explained Le Beau. "The offensive players are taller, and he's underneath them most of the time. Then, with his strength, he can use that to his advantage, and he's got enough speed that they have to honor that, too. He's got the combination of strength and speed, and that's what is unique about James. He never stops on any play, never gives up in any game." People from outside the organization praised Harrison as well. "He is an intense, serious guy with a great appreciation for football history," said former Dallas Cowboy great Troy Aikman. "[He is] consistently motivated to prove himself."

The AFC Central Division champion Steelers entered the 2008 playoffs with swaggering confidence. The team then rolled through the conference playoffs, defeating the San Diego Chargers 35-24 and the Ravens 23-14. The win over Baltimore earned Pittsburgh another trip to the Super Bowl—this time to face a high-scoring Arizona Cardinals team led by quarterback Kurt Warner and wide receiver Larry Fitzgerald.

Harrison (#92) runs for a 100-yard touchdown after intercepting the ball during the Pittsburgh Steelers-Arizona Cardinals Super Bowl game, 2009.

Leading up to the kickoff for Super Bowl XLIII (43) in February 2009, Harrison admitted that he was even more excited than he had been for Super Bowl XL in January 2006. "It means a little bit more to me [this time] because I am a starter instead of playing just on special teams," he explained. "I have matured. I handle situations a lot differently now than I would back then.... I have learned the game and taken time to study the game."

Spectacular Play Leads to Super Bowl Glory

The clash between Pittsburgh and Arizona was tight from the opening kickoff to the final gun, and it made for one of the greatest games in Super Bowl history. The Steelers seemed to have the momentum for most of the first half. But with 18 seconds to go in the half, they were only ahead 10-7 and the Cardinals were poised on Pittsburgh's one-yard line, ready to take the lead.

At that point, though, Harrison made an extraordinary play. Warner tried to hit Arizona receiver Anquan Boldin on a quick pass in the end zone for a touchdown, but Harrison stepped back into the passing lane and picked off the pass. The interception alone was a huge play, but Harrison was not satisfied with just killing the Cardinals drive. Clutching the football in his arms, he rumbled down the sidelines for a 100-yard touchdown return to give the Steelers a 17-7 lead at the half. "I wasn't able to see him around my linemen," Warner said after the game. "He made a great play, not just the interception but to get it in for the touchdown." Harrison's teammates were thrilled—but not all that surprised—at his heroics. "Those are the types of plays he has been making all year," said Steelers quarterback Ben Roethlisberger. "That's the reason why he was the Defensive Player of the Year."

As the second half unfolded, Arizona came storming back on the strength of Warner's arm and Fitzgerald's acrobatic catches. The Cardinals even took a 23-20 lead with less than three minutes to go in the game when Warner hooked up with Fitzgerald on a long touchdown pass. But Pittsburgh's offense responded. Roethlisberger guided the Steelers on an 88-yard game-winning drive. The drive was capped by a touchdown pass to receiver Santonio Holmes in the corner of the end zone in the final seconds of the game.

Afterwards, an exhausted but happy Pittsburgh team basked in the glow of their triumph. Harrison, meanwhile, took great satisfaction in the knowledge that his 100-yard interception return—the longest touchdown in Super Bowl history—had helped lift his team to the championship. "It was tiring," he admitted, "but it was all worth it."

HOME AND FAMILY

Harrison lives in the Pittsburgh area. He has a young son, James Harrison III, with Beth Tibbott. He and Tibbott no longer have a romantic relationship, but she lives close by and Harrison sees his son almost every day. "That's the greatest blessing God has given me," Harrison said. "I'm extremely happy and fortunate to have him."

HOBBIES AND OTHER INTERESTS

Harrison loves to watch classic cartoons like "The Flintstones" and "The Jetsons," as well as adult cartoons like "Family Guy." "That's my thing, man," he said. "I like cartoons. I'll watch just about any cartoon." His other off-the-field interests include fishing.

HONORS AND AWARDS

All-Conference First Team Defense (Mid-American Conference): 2001
NFL Pro Bowl selection: 2007, 2008
Team Most Valuable Player (Pittsburgh Steelers): 2007
NFL All-Pro Team: 2008
NFL Defensive Player of the Year (Associated Press): 2008
NFL Defensive Player of the Year (*Pro Football Weekly*): 2008

FURTHER READING

Periodicals

Akron Beacon Journal, Oct. 9, 2004; Feb. 10, 2008
Beaver County (PA) Times, Aug. 4, 2008
Boston Herald, Jan. 25, 2009
Kansas City Star, Jan. 30, 2009
Los Angeles Times, Jan. 31, 2009, p.D1
New York Times, Dec. 9, 2007, Sports, p.9; Jan. 6, 2009, Sports, p.10; Feb. 2, 2009, Sports, p.3
Pittsburgh Post-Gazette, Dec. 17, 2004; Dec. 27, 2004; Apr. 14, 2006
Sporting News, Dec. 22, 2008; Feb. 2, 2009, p.27
Sports Illustrated, 2009 Commemorative Issue, p.68; Feb. 11, 2009
USA Today, Dec. 1, 2008, p.C4

Online Articles

http://sports.espn.go.com/nfl/playoffs2008/news/story?id=3855349
(ESPN, "Harrison Gives Steelers 'Scary' Presence," Jan. 29, 2009)
http://sports.espn.go.com/espn/page2/story?page=easterbrook/090203&sportCat=nfl
(ESPN, "A Fascinating Super Bowl, from Start to Finish," Feb. 3, 2009)
http://www.sportingnews.com/yourturn/viewtopic.php?t=504045
(Sporting News, "Steelers' Harrison First Undrafted AP Defensive Player of the Year," Jan. 6, 2009)

ADDRESS

James Harrison
Pittsburgh Steelers
P.O. Box 6763
Pittsburgh, PA 15212

WORLD WIDE WEB SITES

http://www.nfl.com
http://www.steelers.com

Jimmie Johnson 1975-

American Professional Race Car Driver
Three-Time NASCAR Sprint Cup Champion

BIRTH

Jimmie Johnson was born on September 17, 1975, in El Cajon,
California. Jimmie is his given name. "My father's best friend
was unfortunately killed when they were teenagers racing
motorcycles, and his name was Jimmie, and they spelled it
with an IE," he explained. "So my dad said then when he had
a son he would name him Jimmie and spell it with an IE."
Jimmie's father, Gary Johnson, operated heavy machinery for

a living. His mother, Cathy Johnson, drove a school bus. Jimmie has two younger brothers, Jarit and Jessie.

YOUTH

Johnson grew up in a double-wide mobile home in El Cajon, a working-class suburb of San Diego. He belonged to a close-knit family that enjoyed spending time in the outdoors, either camping or riding motorcycles. His grandparents owned a motorcycle shop, and he received a little 50cc bike for Christmas when he was four years old. "My parents didn't have the means to buy me anything but motorcycles," he noted. Jimmie started racing on his motorcycle at age five and won his first league championship at age eight.

> *Johnson's father worked as a mechanic on a desert buggy race team, and his son enjoyed hanging out at these events. "He'd drag me to a lot of races, and I'd volunteer to work in the pits, scrape mud off the buggies," Jimmie recalled. "It gave me a chance to get into the pit area and meet other drivers and crew members."*

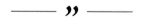

As he got older, Johnson often accompanied his father to off-road auto races. Gary Johnson worked as a mechanic on a desert buggy race team, and his son enjoyed hanging out at these events. "He'd drag me to a lot of races, and I'd volunteer to work in the pits, scrape mud off the buggies," Jimmie recalled. "It gave me a chance to get into the pit area and meet other drivers and crew members."

A polite, curious, and well-spoken young man, Johnson soon talked his way into the driver's seat of a racing buggy. Before he even got his driver's license, he started racing in the Mickey Thompson Stadium Racing Series, which took place on dirt courses set up inside baseball and football stadiums. He also drove buggies in desert races organized by the Short Course Off-Road Enthusiasts (SCORE). His strong performances earned him an opportunity to drive a Chevrolet in the Grand National Truck Series. Johnson won the first of three consecutive truck championships in 1992, at the age of 16.

Throughout his early racing career, Johnson never felt any pressure to win or even to compete. His father just encouraged him and his brothers to do their best. "If we got [done with a race] and we'd tried as hard as we could, he was fine," he remembered. "It didn't matter where we finished. That's something I've been extremely lucky about—that my parents took that approach with us."

Although Johnson showed a great deal of talent as a young racer, he still needed to mature as a driver. For a while, his desire to go fast made him reckless. He learned an important lesson in 1994, during the Baja 1000 endurance race across the Mexican desert. After 20 straight hours of driving, he fell asleep at the wheel and flipped his truck into a sand wash. Luckily, he suffered only minor injuries. But he had two days to sit and think about his mistake before his support crew finally rescued him. "Until that point, I was extremely aggressive, flipping trucks. I tore up a lot of equipment," Johnson acknowledged. "My career was at a critical point there. I was fast and aggressive but I wasn't winning because I was making a lot of mistakes. That low point of almost killing myself in a crash changed me as a driver."

EDUCATION

Johnson graduated from Granite Hills High School in El Cajon in 1993 with a solid B average. He played water polo and competed on the school's swim team.

CAREER HIGHLIGHTS

Becoming a Race Car Driver

After graduating from high school, Johnson worked for a construction company and for a company that made shock absorbers. But his true love was racing, and he hoped to find a way to turn it into a career. In 1996, at the age of 21, he decided to leave California to pursue his dream of becoming a professional racer. He moved across the country to Charlotte, North Carolina—the capital of NASCAR.

The National Association for Stock Car Auto Racing (NASCAR) was founded in 1948. The organization oversaw various racing leagues that had formed throughout the south and applied a common set of rules for tracks, cars, and drivers. One of the main rules of NASCAR was that the racing machines must be "stock cars," based on American-made models sold in automobile dealerships. Over time, though, the base vehicles were modified in many ways to increase performance and safety. As of 2008, NASCAR sanctioned around 1,500 events each year at 100 tracks across the country. Drivers compete in a series of 36 races over the course of the season, and they receive points for the order in which they finish a race. The driver with the most points at the end of the season wins the title.

A view of the action in the pit, during a pit stop in the Napa Auto Parts 500, 2002. Johnson went on to win the race.

NASCAR actually oversees several different levels of racing series. But when people talk about NASCAR, they are usually referring to the most popular NASCAR race series, the Sprint Cup series. (The name of this series has changed over the years: it was known as the Winston Cup until 2004 and the Nextel Cup through 2008, and it's now known as the Sprint Cup.) The Sprint Cup series starts with the Daytona 500 in February in Daytona Beach, Florida, and continues until the Ford 400 in November in Homestead, Florida; other big races include the Brickyard 400 at the Indianapolis Motor Speedway and the Coca-Cola 600 at Lowes Motor Speedway near Charlotte, North Carolina.

When Johnson traveled to Charlotte, he was determined to become a NASCAR driver. Once he arrived, he set about making contacts among NASCAR crew members, drivers, and car owners in hopes of eventually working his way up to the Sprint Cup series. He hung around places frequented by racers, looking for opportunities to introduce himself, shake hands, and ask for advice. "I would go to places where I knew crew guys ate lunch and I'd sit there all through lunch just trying to meet people," he recalled.

Johnson's persistence paid off in 1997, when he was offered a chance to compete in the American Speed Association (ASA) AC Delco Challenge short-track series. Since he had always raced on dirt tracks, he initially struggled to adjust to pavement. In fact, he spun out 12 times in his first race. He learned quickly, though, and soon established himself as a talented young driver. During the 1998 season Johnson finished fourth in the ASA national championship point standings and earned Rookie of the Year honors. The following year he won two races and moved up to third in the point standings.

Breaking into NASCAR

Johnson's strong performance in the ASA short-course series earned him an opportunity to compete in the Nationwide Series (formerly known as the Busch Grand National Series), which is considered the second tier of NASCAR racing behind the Sprint Cup. He started three Nationwide races in 1998 and five the following year, while also competing in the ASA series. In 2000 Johnson moved up to compete in the Nationwide Series on a full-time basis. He finished in the top 10 in six different events to end the season ranked 10th in the point standings. In 2001 Johnson won his first Nationwide Series race, at Chicagoland Speedway, on his way to an eighth-place finish in the point standings. He also made his first appearance in the prestigious Sprint Cup Series that October, qualifying 15th and finishing 39th at Lowe's Motor Speedway in Charlotte.

> *Johnson was a reckless driver when he was young, until he flipped his truck during a race in the Mexican desert and had to wait two days for someone to rescue him.*
> "Until that point, I was extremely aggressive, flipping trucks. I tore up a lot of equipment," he acknowledged. "My career was at a critical point there. I was fast and aggressive but I wasn't winning because I was making a lot of mistakes. That low point of almost killing myself in a crash changed me as a driver."

Around that time, Johnson learned that the corporate sponsor of his Nationwide Series car planned to end its relationship with NASCAR. With his ride in jeopardy, he decided to approach a fellow driver for advice. He knocked on the motor home of Jeff Gordon—another young driver from California who had already won three Winston Cup championships and would win a fourth that year—and asked him what his next career move should be. "I went to Jeff and said, 'Hey, do you have any advice?'" John-

———— " ————

"He impressed me," Jeff Gordon said about meeting Johnson. "He was the guy I wanted. We hit it off from the beginning. I knew that's why he'd fit so well. I knew it was going to be a team that was under the same roof as the 24 [Gordon's car] and that those people had to work really well together and the drivers had to work really close together."

———— " ————

son remembered. "He said, 'You're not gonna believe this, but we're interested in starting a fourth Winston Cup team in 2002, and we want you to possibly drive that car.' I was like, 'What did you say?' It was so amazing to go in looking for some advice and walk out of the back of that truck thinking I might have a shot at a Winston Cup ride."

After discussing the choice with Rick Hendrick, team owner of Hendrick Motorsports, Gordon made Johnson an offer to drive the team's fourth car, which he co-owned. Many NASCAR analysts and fans were shocked by the move. Since Gordon and Hendrick could have had their pick among the best racers available, they wondered why they chose a young, unknown, unproven driver like Johnson. "He impressed me," Gordon explained. "He was the guy I wanted. We hit it off from the beginning. I knew that's why he'd fit so well. I knew it was going to be a team that was under the same roof as the 24 [Gordon's car] and that those people had to work really well together and the drivers had to work really close together."

Joining the Hendrick Motorsports Team

When Johnson joined Hendrick Motorsports, he became part of one of the largest and most successful teams in NASCAR history. Hendrick's resources included 500 employees, a brand-new race shop with state-of-the-art technology, and a friendly, cooperative atmosphere among the race teams. "All four cars are an open book to one another from Daytona testing [prior to the start of the Cup season] all the way to the final laps at Homestead [the last race of the year]," said Steve Letarte, Gordon's crew chief. "We share air pressures during the race, pit strategies, setup information all weekend long."

Johnson's new car was the number 48 Chevrolet sponsored by Lowe's home improvement stores. "There were numbers to choose from, and 48

Johnson is shown here with Jeff Gordon, who helped him get his start in NASCAR and who is part owner of his car.

was one of them," he recalled. "I've had a lot of success through the years with the number 4 and the number 8, and it all fit in place with the 24 car and Jeff owning a part of the team I was driving."

Johnson soon proved that the team's confidence in him was well-founded. He burst onto the Winston Cup scene in 2002 by qualifying on the pole (in the first position) at the season-opening Daytona 500. He finished among the top 10 six times in his first 12 races in NASCAR's top series. He managed to win his first Winston Cup race—the NAPA Auto Parts 500 in Fontana, California—in just his 13th career start.

Johnson's strong early-season performance made him the first rookie driver ever to sit atop the Winston Cup point standings. (Drivers receive points based on their finish position in each race. The winning driver is awarded 182 points, and the number of points awarded drops gradually for each lower finish position. Competitors can also earn up to 10 bonus points per race: 5 for any driver who leads a lap; and 5 for the driver who leads the most laps.) Johnson ended his spectacular rookie season with three victories and a fifth-place finish in the point standings. "Rick was happy, Lowe's was thrilled, and I was breathing a little easier," Gordon recalled. "Having Jimmie perform so well eliminated a lot of worry."

Johnson was pleased with his instant success at NASCAR's highest level, although he was taken aback by the sudden increase in attention and demands on his time. "I'm used to sitting around, hanging with the guys, talking about setups, and now there are 200 people outside saying your name and trying to get autographs," he noted. "It really cuts into some of that downtime I was used to having."

> "It was just a great year for the entire Lowe's team. We have a great relationship, great equipment, and great sponsors.... I'm so fortunate to have the crew that I do. They've made a sophomore finish second this year," Johnson said after the 2003 season. "If you look at history, it usually takes three, four, or five years to get the driver and the team into championship form. Maybe next year will be that special year for us."

Falling Just Short of a Title

Over the next three seasons, Johnson consistently ranked among the top Cup competitors. Each year, however, he fell just short of earning enough points to claim the championship. In 2003 Johnson posted three victories and 14 top-5 finishes, to end the season ranked second in the point standings. It was a remarkable performance for a second-year driver. "It was just a great year for the entire Lowe's team. We have a great relationship, great equipment, and great sponsors.... I'm so fortunate to have the crew that I do. They've made a sophomore finish second this year," he said afterward. "If you look at history, it usually takes three, four, or five years to get the driver and the team into championship form. Maybe next year will be that special year for us."

Prior to the start of the 2004 season, NASCAR changed the system that determined which driver earned the coveted Cup points title. Instead of simply adding up each driver's points at the end of the 36-race season, the organization instituted a 10-race playoff called the Chase for the Cup. Only the top 12 drivers in the point standings at the end of 26 races qualified to compete in the Chase. The 12 qualifiers had their points reset to 5,000, and they also received 10 additional points for each victory they had

Johnson and the 48 Chevrolet at Daytona in 2004.

registered during the season's first 26 races. During the 10-race Chase, points were awarded as usual. This system effectively wiped out any big point leads that a driver may have accumulated, making the end of the season more exciting for fans.

Johnson started out strong in 2004 and led the point standings by mid-season. But he hit a rough patch from August to October that dropped him all the way down to ninth place, 247 points behind the leader. "I didn't feel [the championship hopes] were over, but I'm a realist and I knew it was out of our control," he said. "We were going to need mistakes made by everybody ahead of us to catch up." Johnson launched an amazing come-back, winning four of the last six races of the year. Unfortunately, his eight victories and 14 top-5 finishes were not quite good enough to win the title. In the closest points race in Cup history, he finished second to Kurt Busch by eight points. "It showed me at the end of the year that you can't give up until the last lap," he noted.

The 2005 season proved to be a difficult one for Johnson. Although he led the point standings for half the year, he hit another rough patch in late summer that saw him drop to sixth place. During this period—for the first time in his Cup career—he was involved in a couple of on-track incidents that drew criticism from fellow drivers. "It makes me think harder about who I am, what I am, and the type of driver I am," he said of this experience. "I'm not going to let anybody's opinion change what I do or who I am." As in previous years, Johnson worked his way back up in the standings and entered the final race of the Chase in second place. Unfortunately, a blown tire knocked him out of the race early and dropped him to fifth in points for the season.

Although Johnson ended 2005 with a respectable four victories and 13 top-5 finishes, it was a low point in his career. He and his crew had failed to perform up to expectations, and they felt deeply disappointed. Johnson and his chief, Chad Knaus, took out their frustrations on each other. The situation became so bad that the team owner had to step in to offer some perspective. "I think we had so much built up on the early success that we had had and we were so frustrated with the fact we hadn't won, that we were fighting like cats and dogs," Johnson remembered. "Mr. Hendrick is a great people person, and can really relate to anybody in any situation. And we were acting like kids, so he sat us down like kids, and had a gallon of milk, some Mickey Mouse plates with cookies, … and said, 'All right, guys, if you are going to act like this, then I will treat you like this.' And, you know, we hashed out the issues that were bothering us, and then won every championship since."

Winning the Nextel Cup

As the 2006 Cup season approached, Johnson and his crew were prepared to do everything possible to claim the elusive championship. Just prior to the first race of the year—the fabled Daytona 500—crew chief Chad Knaus came under criticism for going too far in his efforts to win. A pre-race technical inspection revealed that some parts of Johnson's car had been modified in ways that were not allowed under NASCAR rules. The illegal modifications resulted in Knaus being suspended for the race. Johnson overcame this setback and won his first Daytona 500. "We play within a set of rules. Chad broke the rules. He's admitted that. We're serving our penalty," he said afterward. "We stepped up today and won the biggest race in our sport, and that is something I am so proud of."

Johnson continued to run well for much of the 2006 season, leading the point standings for 22 weeks. Following his usual pattern, however, he experienced a late-season slump in which he placed 10th or lower in nine straight races. He qualified for the Chase for the Cup, but his chances of claiming the title looked slim. "We're pretty far out, and it's going to be tough to make up the deficit that we have," he acknowledged. "But the way this Chase has started and the way every year the Chase has been that I've been a part of it, it's so unpredictable. Anything can happen."

Sure enough, Johnson came charging back into contention during the Chase. He soared up the standings over a six-race stretch, enabling him to reclaim the top position by the time the series entered the final race of the season in Homestead, Florida. He only needed to finish 12th or better in this event to capture his first Cup championship. Just 16 laps into the Homestead race, though, a spring broke off a competitor's car and flew through Johnson's window, hitting him in the nose. His crew managed to fix him up during the next pit stop, but he lost so much time that he dropped back to 40th place in the race. He moved steadily through the field over the next 60 laps, however, and finished ninth—well enough to claim his first Nextel Cup title by 56 points over Matt Kenseth. "It may take a while to sink in. I knew we had a great team. I knew all along we could do it," he declared. "I've won a lot of big, big events, and they're very special. But there's nothing like a championship. There's nothing like having that respect through the garage, in the media, with the fans, of being THE guy." Johnson ended the season with 5 victories and 13 top-5 finishes, and he was named Driver of the Year by NASCAR.

> *"It may take a while to sink in.," Johnson said about winning the Cup in 2006. "I knew we had a great team. I knew all along we could do it. I've won a lot of big, big events, and they're very special. But there's nothing like a championship. There's nothing like having that respect through the garage, in the media, with the fans, of being THE guy."*

Winning Three Consecutive Championships

Johnson was not satisfied with one championship, however. As the 2007 season got underway, he expressed determination to defend his title. "To be a repeat champion puts you in the top of our sport," he stated. "I want

Johnson (#48) and Dale Earnhardt Jr. (#8) battle for position.

to be in that elite status of guys." Johnson looked unstoppable at the beginning of the year, posting four victories in the first 10 races. But then he entered a slump in which he went 14 races without a win. This dry spell coincided with Knaus serving another suspension from NASCAR for making illegal modifications to the fenders of the 48 car.

Once again, though, Johnson made a terrific comeback during the Chase. He won four races in a row at the end of the season to earn a second consecutive championship by 77 points over Gordon, his mentor and car owner. "He's been the best in the sport, and it means a lot to me to beat Jeff Gordon when he's on his game and as competitive as he was last year. I'm really proud of that," Johnson said afterward. "In some ways it's difficult because he's a great friend and I'd love to see him as a five-time champion. So I had mixed emotions, but it was just a great battle through the whole season."

Johnson thus became the first driver to repeat as Cup champion since Gordon achieved the feat in the 1997 and 1998 seasons. In addition, his 10 race wins marked the first time any driver had posted double-digit victories in a season since Gordon had done so in 1998. In recognition of his efforts, Johnson received NASCAR's Driver of the Year Award for the second time. "Winning back-to-back championships is something I'm very, very proud of," he stated. "The good thing, I feel, is that we're just hitting our stride. I think we have a lot of good years ahead of us, and we'll be fighting for more championships and certainly winning more races as years go by. Hopefully we can be a three-time champion in the near future."

Johnson started out slowly during the 2008 season, but he improved steadily and looked strong toward the end. He went on to dominate the Chase, winning three races and posting eight finishes in the top 10. By the time the series reached the final race at Homestead, Johnson held an almost-insurmountable lead of 141 points. Needing to finish only 36th to claim a third straight title, he raced conservatively and avoided trouble. Johnson ended the season with 7 wins and 15 top-5 finishes to earn the championship by 69 points over Carl Edwards. He thus tied the legendary Cale Yarborough—who won titles in 1976, 1977, and 1978—as the only drivers in NASCAR's 60-year history to "threepeat." He also won his third straight Driver of the Year Award. "It's been an amazing run. I've worked all my life to get here, but I never could have dreamed of winning three championships in a row," Johnson said afterward. "We'll enjoy it for a little while, then we'll start working on getting number four."

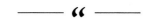

"It's been an amazing run. I've worked all my life to get here, but I never could have dreamed of winning three championships in a row," Johnson said afterward. *"We'll enjoy it for a little while, then we'll start working on getting number four."*

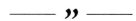

Building a Dynasty

Through the end of the 2008 season, Johnson's career statistics included 40 race wins (placing him third among active drivers), 101 finishes in the top 5, and 156 finishes in the top 10 in 255 Cup starts. Showing remarkable consistency, he ranked among the top 5 in the point standings at the end of every Cup season in his seven-year career. Johnson also showed an amazing ability to turn in his best performances in important races. Out of the 50 Chase races held since 2004, he won 14—8 more than any other driver. His success helped him earn $23 million in prize money and endorsements in 2008 alone. "I'm so far ahead of the goals and dreams I set that this is all icing on the cake," he noted.

Johnson always made sure to give Hendrick Motorsports, Chad Knaus, and his whole crew equal credit for the performance of the 48 Chevrolet.

97

"Chad is real aggressive and is not afraid to make the tough call and put a lot of pressure on everyone around him," said fellow driver Jeff Burton. "They're a team with swagger. They're willing to make that gamble of possibly giving up a fifth place for a win." "The way you win championships in the Chase era is to use the first 26 races to get ready for the last 10, and Jimmie and Chad do that better than anyone else," added NASCAR analyst Darrell Waltrip. "They have as much engineering support at Hendrick Motorsports as anyone in the sport. Heck, I don't see why they can't win a fourth straight championship next season."

———— **"** ————

Johnson's story demonstrates that an unknown driver might just have the ability to make it big in racing. "A lot of it is who you know," he said. "A lot of people are bashful about introducing themselves, writing letters, approaching people. It's a touchy thing to do. You can definitely wear out your welcome. But if you show that enthusiasm and determination and you have some talent, you're going to get a shot."

———— **"** ————

While Johnson has emerged as the top driver on the Hendrick Motorsports team, he has remained close friends with Jeff Gordon. "I don't think many people could handle that situation better than he and I do," Gordon acknowledged. "I am happy for him, he's happy for me, but we also know how bad we want it for ourselves and our teams." Gordon has found himself in the unlikely position of studying his teammate's car and driving style for clues about how to improve his own performance. "Every time he's blistering fast, I say, 'Put that setup in,' and then I'm absolutely terrible," Gordon noted. "I know what's under their car, and I always shake my head. I don't know how they make that work. But Jimmie's driving style is different enough that it does."

Despite his three consecutive Cup championships, Johnson is not as popular with NASCAR fans as a number of less accomplished drivers. Some fans seem to resent the way that he and his well-funded Hendrick Motorsports team have dominated the sport in recent years. Others seem to find him bland and boring compared to the colorful personalities exhibited by some other drivers. After all, Johnson does not make many controversial statements to reporters, and he generally avoids becoming involved in conflicts or feuds with other drivers. "He doesn't have Tony Stewart's

*Johnson (front right) leading the pack at the start of this 2008 race—
and leading the way to his third consecutive title.*

flame-throwing personality, but he's not an introvert," said team owner
Rick Hendrick. "He's got as many friends or more than any other driver.
He's got friends he went to school with, friends he raced with, and movie-
star friends, and when they come together, he's the same with all of them.
He's a fun-loving guy who plays as hard as he races."

Johnson's many friends rush to defend him from critics who say he is dull.
"He's probably one of the best guys in the world and one of the most talented guys in the garage," said longtime friend Casey Mears. "At the same
time, he's probably more easy to approach and more human than most.
Jimmie's just a good guy." Still, Johnson admits that he sometimes has
trouble letting his true self show through to fans. "I can be freaking out inside, but then I open my mouth and I sound calm. I don't know where this
device comes from," he explained. "It helps me in racing because you
never want to lose your cool, but it's also probably kept people from getting to know the real me."

Thanks to his incredible success on the track, the man who once knocked
hopefully on the door to Jeff Gordon's trailer now has other people approaching him for advice on breaking into NASCAR. His own story
demonstrates that an unknown driver might just have the ability to make
it big in racing. "A lot of it is who you know," he said. "A lot of people are
bashful about introducing themselves, writing letters, approaching people.

It's a touchy thing to do. You can definitely wear out your welcome. But if you show that enthusiasm and determination and you have some talent, you're going to get a shot."

MARRIAGE AND FAMILY

Johnson met his future wife, model Chandra Janway, at a party in New York City in 2002. He proposed to her a year later while they were skiing at Beaver Creek, Colorado. They were married on December 11, 2004, on the tropical island of St. Barts in the Caribbean. They have a 12,000-square-foot house in Mooresville, North Carolina, as well as a loft apartment in the Chelsea neighborhood of Manhattan in New York City. "Having Chandi in my life allows me not to worry about things outside of racing when I walk through the gates each weekend," Johnson stated. "This sounds corny, but Chandi and I are teammates. We're in love, and she gives me total peace of mind."

Johnson also remains close to his family. In fact, his father drives his million-dollar motor home from track to track throughout the NASCAR race season and often serves as a spotter in the stands during races.

HOBBIES AND OTHER INTERESTS

In his spare time, Johnson enjoys watching football, playing golf, and going downhill skiing and snowboarding. He also spends a lot of time cruising around Lake Norman in his 35-foot Fountain powerboat. "I love to be out on the water, going fast!" he admitted.

Johnson is deeply committed to charity work. "Chandra and I have been very blessed," he noted. "We get to do what we enjoy in life, and that is something we don't take for granted. We have incredibly supportive friends and family, and we feel that I have the best fans in our sport. It is in that spirit of thankfulness that we launched the Jimmie Johnson Foundation in February 2006."

The foundation works primarily to help families and children in need. It brings critically ill fans to NASCAR races through the Make-a-Wish Foundation, builds homes for deserving families in El Cajon through Habitat for Humanity, and sponsors Jimmie Johnson's Victory Lanes bowling alley at Kyle Petty's Victory Junction Camp for children with serious illnesses or chronic medical conditions. Johnson finds it very gratifying to give something back. "I am consumed with competition and success. You start using those as benchmarks for happiness," he acknowledged. "[But] when you see someone fighting for their life, the fact that they're smiling and they're happy, it just re-racks your brain."

HONORS AND AWARDS

Rookie of the Year (American Speed Association): 1998
NASCAR Driver of the Year: 2006, 2007, 2008
NASCAR Nextel/Sprint Cup Championship: 2006, 2007, 2008

FURTHER READING

Books

LeMasters, Ron Jr. *Jimmie Johnson: A Desert Rat's Race to NASCAR Stardom,* 2004
Gitlin, Marty. *Jimmie Johnson: Racing Champ,* 2008

Periodicals

New York Times, Nov. 19, 2008, p.B15
Sports Illustrated, Dec. 1, 2002, p.70; Nov. 26, 2007, p.54; Nov. 24, 2008, p.30
Sports Illustrated for Kids, Nov. 1, 2005, p.53; Feb. 2008, p.28
USA Today, Sep. 12, 2007, p.C1; Nov. 15, 2007, p.C1; Oct. 15, 2008, p.C8; Nov. 12, 2008, p.C1

Online Article

http://signonsandiego.com
("See How Far Jimmie Johnson Has Come from El Cajon," *San Diego Union-Tribune,* Feb. 20, 2005)

ADDRESS

Jimmie Johnson
Jimmie Johnson Fan Club
4325 Papa Joe Hendrick Blvd.
Charlotte, NC 28262

WORLD WIDE WEB SITES

http://www.jimmiejohnson.com
http://www.hendrickmotorsports.com
http://www.lowesracing.com
http://www.nascar.com/drivers
http://www.jimmiejohnsonfoundation.org

Demi Lovato 1992-

American Singer and Actress
Star of *Camp Rock*, "Sonny With a Chance," and
Princess Protection Program

BIRTH

Demi Lovato was born Demetria Devonne Lovato on August 20, 1992, in Dallas, Texas. Her parents, Patrick and Dianna, are divorced. Dianna, a former professional cheerleader and country singer, is currently married to Eddie De La Garza, a car dealership manager who is Lovato's stepfather and co-manager. Lovato has two siblings—an older sister, Dallas, and a younger sister, Madison. Lovato is of Hispanic, Irish, and Italian descent.

Lovato appeared on "Barney and Friends" as Barney's friend Angela.

YOUTH AND EDUCATION

Lovato learned a great deal about show business from her mother. Before having children, Dianna was a professional cheerleader for the Dallas Cowboys and then a country-western singer. She once opened a show at Six Flags for country stars Reba McEntire and George Strait, an achievement Lovato has proudly recounted in interviews.

Lovato's parents divorced in 1994, when Demi was about two. After the divorce her father moved to New Mexico, and since then he has had little contact with her. Her mother soon remarried, and Demi's stepfather helped raise her from an early age. Eddie and Dianna helped cultivate Lovato's interest in singing and acting. An early experience in a kindergarten talent show introduced her to the spotlight. She dared to sing a difficult number, "My Heart Will Go On" by Celine Dion, and forgot the words. Still, she was so thrilled to perform that she eagerly hoped for more opportunities like that one.

Dianna began arranging auditions for the aspiring young star. When she was six years old, Lovato was selected to join a cast of young actors on

"Barney and Friends," a children's show featuring a friendly purple dinosaur. Lovato appeared as Barney's friend Angela for two seasons. That's when she became good friends with one of her co-stars, Selena Gomez, who remembered the moment like this: "It was scorching hot, July. We were in line with 1,400 kids and we happened to be standing right next to each other. She had a little bow in her hair, and she turned around and she looked at me and said, "Do you want to color?' … After that we had a couple of callbacks, and I saw her from the other side of the room and it was kind of a movie moment. We still joke about it. We were inseparable after doing two seasons together, and our moms are best friends now." (For more information on Gomez, see *Biography Today*, Sep. 2008.)

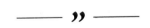

Lovato struggled to cope with being bullied by her classmates. The bullying became so intense that she asked her mother to be home schooled. "I asked to leave public school," she revealed. "I was kind of bullied. I had a hate wall in the bathroom, and everyone signed a petition that said 'We all hate Demi Lovato.'"

Dealing with Bullying

Lovato was only seven when she started playing the piano. Taking encouragement from her mother, she also started to write songs. She naturally wasn't ready for the challenges of songwriting at such a young age. However, after a few years she realized that writing songs was a great way to express her pain and other feelings. While Lovato was attending middle school in Texas, she began having problems with bullies.

Lovato struggled to cope with being bullied by her classmates. The bullying became so intense that she asked her mother to be home schooled. "I asked to leave public school," she revealed. "I was kind of bullied. I had a hate wall in the bathroom, and everyone signed a petition that said 'We all hate Demi Lovato.'" She didn't understand why her classmates were attacking her like that. "They would text me and say, 'We're going to make your life a living hell.' I remember asking them, 'What did I do?' and no one could answer.... [One day] some of the girls were threatening to beat me up. They chased me into a bathroom upstairs. I hid. I was crying, and I called my mom, and I said, 'You need to take me out of school. I hate my life here.'" Her mother picked her up, and since then she has been home schooled. Since that difficult time, songwriting has served as a great outlet for her. "I've written probably around like 200, 300 songs," she said. "It's kind of like therapy for me. It is what I do in my spare time and I can't live without it."

Being home schooled suited Lovato. It allowed her to avoid the bullies, and she now had a schedule that let her audition for several television shows. Although she secured a small role on an episode of the TV drama "Prison Break," steady parts were hard to come by, and she became frustrated. "After hundreds of auditions and nothing, you're sitting home and wondering, 'What am I doing?'" she remembered.

CAREER HIGHLIGHTS

Breaking into Disney

When a Disney Channel talent search came to Dallas, Lovato agreed to try out. This time, the network was looking for actors for "As the Bell Rings," a TV series set to air in 2007 as five-minute segments between regular programs. Lovato was very nervous during the audition. "Even though the show was only, like five minutes, it was the Disney Channel!" she recalled. "I thought it was the coolest thing." But she was able to keep enough composure to land the part. "When I got the part, I actually cried," she admitted. "I thought, 'I'm not going to be able to do this—I'm not funny! I'm never going to be able to work for the Disney Channel, because they're based on comedy."

With the exposure from "As the Bell Rings," Lovato and her family were hoping for a big break. The perfect opportunity came when Disney announced openings for parts on an upcoming TV show. The series would star the wildly popular Jonas Brothers. By that point the rock trio—composed of Joe, Kevin, and Nick—had already achieved platinum album sales. (For more information on the Jonas Brothers, see *Biography Today*, Jan. 2008.) Lovato didn't land a regular role on "Jonas Brothers: Living the Dream," but her audition made a strong enough impression to ensure more auditions.

The Disney network next asked Lovato to audition for a part in the soon-to-be-filmed *Camp Rock*, a TV musical to feature the Jonas Brothers. She arrived at the audition prepared only to showcase her acting skills, but one executive at the meeting, Disney Channel Worldwide president Gary Marsh, asked to hear her singing voice. She obliged by launching into "Ain't No Other Man" by Christina Aguilera. "Our jaws just dropped," remembered Hollywood Records senior vice president and general manager Bob Cavallo. Lovato won the part in *Camp Rock*, plus Disney also signed her to Hollywood Records, the music label famous for breaking the Jonas Brothers, Hillary Duff, and Miley Cyrus. (For more information on Cyrus, see *Biography Today*, Sep. 2007; for Duff, see *Biography Today*, Sep. 2002.)

Camp Rock

In August 2007, Lovato began filming *Camp Rock* at a location in Canada, outside Toronto, Ontario. The movie was full of singing and dancing, much like the 2006 Disney blockbuster *High School Musical.* Lovato played Mitchie Torres, who like herself is a singer-songwriter. She hopes to shine at the rock camp but feels held back by her humble background. Her male counterpart is Shane Gray (played by Joe Jonas), a rock star who is forced to work as a camp instructor to clean up his ailing public image. Mitchie attends the camp at a discounted price and on the condition that she work in the camp's kitchen, where her mother is the head cook. She soon makes the mistake of lying about her background in hopes of fitting in with the popular kids.

Lovato performs in several of the musical's numbers, one of which is a stirring duet with Joe Jonas called "This Is Me." The song is about Mitchie's realization that she needs to drop her false façade and be herself. Gary Marsh saw a strong connection between the character and Lovato. "She was going through this same evolution as a human being at the same time as the character," he said. "When she sings 'This Is Me' in the end, this is just not Mitchie, this is Demi telling the world 'This is me.' This was literally her journey coming forward."

"When I got the part, I actually cried," Lovato said about auditioning for "As the Bell Rings." "I thought, 'I'm not going to be able to do this—I'm not funny! I'm never going to be able to work for the Disney Channel, because they're based on comedy."

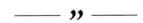

The filming schedule was taxing for the actors, but Lovato took it in stride. One scene, which featured the final dance number "We Rock," took three long days to shoot. For Lovato, the challenge was keeping up a presentable appearance on camera. "I got my hair blown dry six times in one day," she remembered. "You're dancing so much, and you just don't want to glisten like that on camera!"

Camp Rock was a hit when it first aired in June 2008. Shown on several networks, including Disney and ABC, the movie reached 69.5 million viewers worldwide. The soundtrack CD to the film, released the same month, was a success as well, debuting on the *Billboard* Top 200 at No. 3. The single for "This Is Me" claimed the No. 2 spot on the Hot Digital Songs chart.

Scenes from Camp Rock, *including Lovato with the Jonas Brothers at the movie premier.*

The "Burning Up" Tour

While *Camp Rock* was introducing millions of viewers and listeners to Lovato, concert promoters were planning a nationwide tour for her with the Jonas Brothers. The "Burning Up" tour, featuring Lovato as a special guest, made perfect sense because the two acts shared a similar fan base. In addition, Lovato and the brothers had also become good friends and likely would make good tour mates. Before hitting the road, Lovato and the brothers collaborated in the studio to record her debut album. In the world of teen pop music, records are typically manufactured by seasoned professionals, with the young stars doing little behind-the-scenes work. These young musicians, however, proved to be the exception, handling the songwriting and recording duties themselves. Lovato wrote or co-wrote all but two of the songs, and the brothers co-wrote or co-produced a good chunk of the album.

The final dance number in Camp Rock *took three long days to shoot. For Lovato, the challenge was keeping up a presentable appearance on camera. "I got my hair blown dry six times in one day," she remembered. "You're dancing so much, and you just don't want to glisten like that on camera!"*

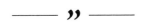

If there was any doubt that Lovato had made it, thousands of screaming fans attending the sold-out "Burning Up" tour served as proof. Running from July to September, the tour hit 56 cities in the United States and Canada. Lovato's show debuted songs from her upcoming album and exhibited her talents as a multi-instrumentalist.

Lovato hardly expected to celebrate her sweet 16 in a strange city and in the middle of a rock tour, but that is where she found herself on August 20. It was difficult being away from most of her family, although she still enjoyed the company of her stepfather, who traveled with her as her co-manager. Concertgoers, of course, were eager to wish her a happy 16th birthday. "Everyone was singing happy birthday to me—and by everyone, I mean 20,000 people at my concert," Lovato recalled. It was clearly a turning point for the teen star. "That was the moment when I said, 'Wow, my life is not the same, but it's even better.'"

Lovato's first album, titled *Don't Forget,* was the commercial hit that she had hoped for. It debuted at No. 2 on the *Billboard* Top 200, selling almost 90,000 copies in the first week of the album's release. It was also the most down-loaded album on iTunes. *Don't Forget* scored well with critics and fans alike. Writing in *Entertainment Weekly,* Leah Greenblatt said that Lovato's album, "while full of catchy choruses, abandons the usual tinkly teen-pop tropes for meaty guitars and percussion; the raucous lead single "Get Back" is more Benatar than Backstreet." Newspaper reviewer Christopher Tessmer wrote, "While Lovato's 11 tracks are polished and hungry for mainstream radio, you can hear the raw emotion and vocal talent in every song."

Several critics noted that Lovato distinguished herself from other teen stars because she wrote much of her own material. They also noted their surprise that Lovato rocked harder than other starlets did. "People have definitely said they weren't expecting the album to be as rock as it is," she explained. "They were expecting the butterfly pop stuff."

> "People have definitely said they weren't expecting the album to be as rock as it is," Lovato said about her debut album, **Don't Forget.** "They were expecting the butterfly pop stuff."

"Sonny With a Chance"

As the album hit the stores, Lovato began preparing for the next major venture: her own Disney sitcom. In "Sonny With a Chance," she stars as Sonny Munroe, a girl from Wisconsin who wins a nationwide search to be the next star of the sketch-comedy show "So Random!" Sonny faces many challenges adapting to the Hollywood lifestyle, including repeated clashes with fellow "So Random!" star Tawni (Tiffany Thornton) and an ongoing rivalry with the cast of "MacKenzie Falls," a soap opera that shoots on the next stage.

Those familiar with Lovato's career so far could identify the similarities between her and Sonny. Lovato's success also required her to move to Hollywood with her family. Such a transition made the sitcom character a natural fit for her. "She's faced with all these obstacles she has to go through to adapt to the Hollywood lifestyle," Lovato said. "My life kind of mirrors it."

Even after her successful turn in *Camp Rock,* Lovato found starring in a TV show—particularly a comedy—a daunting task. Since early childhood, she has considered acting a greater challenge than singing or playing music. But on the set of "Sonny With a Chance" she found the confidence she

*Lovato (Sonny, right) with co-star Tiffany Thornton (Tawni)
in a scene from the first episode of "Sonny With a Chance."*

needed. "I've really let loose and totally had fun with it," she said. Her comfort on camera certainly contributed to the show's success. The first airing of "Sonny With a Chance" drew 4.1 million viewers and proved to be a huge hit with young teens.

Princess Protection Program

In 2009, Lovato appeared in the Disney TV movie *Princess Protection Program.* She was lucky to be able to co-star with her longtime real-life best friend, Selena Gomez, now appearing as the star of the hit comedy TV series "Wizards of Waverly Place." The two had a lot of fun making the movie. They filmed in Costa Rica, where they had sleepovers most nights at their hotel. "We don't really think of it as work," Lovato said.

In the movie, an evil dictator overtakes the tiny country of Costa Luna. The princess Rosalinda Marie Montoya Fiore (played by Lovato) was soon to become the country's ruler. She is rescued by an agent of the secret international agency Princess Protection Program. The agent takes the princess to a PPP base where she is given a new identity, Rosie Gonzalez, then takes her home to live with his family in rural Louisiana. His daughter Carter (played by Gomez) is shocked to learn that she will have to share her bed-

Lovato (Rosie) with her best friend, Selena Gomez (Carter), in a scene from Princess Protection Program.

room with Rosie, who is posing as Carter's cousin. Even worse, Rosie will be enrolling at Carter's school. Despite some conflict at the beginning, the two learn to help each other.

Lovato was able to continue to build her singing career with this movie also. Two of her songs were included in the movie: "One and the Same," a duet with Gomez, and "Two Worlds Collide," a cut from her debut album.

Lovato hopes that her successes so far mark the beginning of a long career that combines both singing and acting. "I plan on doing this for the rest of my life," she said. For upcoming musical projects, she plans a follow-up album, which she predicted would be more soulful and bluesy than her debut, and a subsequent tour. For upcoming acting projects, fans of *Camp Rock* were happy to hear news that Disney is preparing a sequel, for which Lovato, the Jonas Brothers, and the rest of the cast plan to reprise their roles. Production for the sequel will begin in 2009.

HOME AND FAMILY

Lovato enjoys a close bond with her family. While her parents are very protective of their daughter—a necessity for virtually any young superstar—Lovato does not consider them overbearing. She sees her mother as a best friend, and the time on the road spent with her stepfather has drawn them a lot closer. "We have a lot of trust in each other," she said of both her parents.

HOBBIES AND OTHER INTERESTS

Lovato's experiences with bullying have inspired her to advocate for other vulnerable children and teens. In October 2008 Love Our Children USA announced that she, the singer JoJo, and several other stars would participate in the STOMP Out Bullying awareness campaign. Lovato signed up to appear in commercials and on posters. She hoped her contribution would help those girls her age and younger who were not as fortunate as she was to find a solution. "I want to help with bullying because there are girls who can't just up and home-school and focus on their career," she said.

SELECTED CREDITS

Television

"Barney and Friends," 2004
"As the Bell Rings," 2007
Camp Rock, 2008
"Jonas Brothers: Living the Dream," 2008
Princess Protection Program, 2009
"Sonny With a Chance," 2009

Recordings

Don't Forget, 2008

Films

Jonas Brothers: The 3D Concert Experience, 2009

FURTHER READING

Periodicals

Boston Globe, Sep. 23, 2008
Entertainment Weekly, June 6, 2008, p.41; Oct. 3, 2008, p.44; Nov. 21, 2008p.84; Jan. 23, 2009, p.38
Girls' Life, June/July 2008, p.86; Feb./Mar. 2009, p.44
Houston Chronicle, June 20, 2008, p.2
Orlando Sentinel, Feb. 7, 2009
People, Apr. 13, 2009, p.121; July 2009 (Special Edition, multiple articles)
Scholastic Choices, Apr.-May 2009, p.3
Scholastic Scope, Jan. 19, 2009, p.13

USA Today, Jan. 1, 2009; Feb. 3, 2009, p.D8
Washington Post, June 21, 2008

Online Articles

http://www.mtv.com
(MTV, "Demi Lovato Calls on Jonas Brothers for Help with Debut LP,
Onstage Tumble," Aug. 28, 2008; "Demi Lovato Says She Relates to Her
'Sonny With a Chance' Character," Jan. 23, 2009; "Demi Lovato Looking
to Have 'John Mayerish' Songs on New Album," Jan. 27, 2009; "Demi
Lovato: 'I Feel Bad for Miley!'" Feb. 2, 2009; "Demi Lovato Wants to Be
'Funnier' in 'Camp Rock' Sequel," Feb. 27, 2009)
http://www.reuters.com
(Reuters, "'Camp Rock' Sets the Stage for Newcomer Demi Lovato,"
June 15, 2008)
http://www.tvweek.com
(TV Week, "'Sonny' Lights Up Sunday for Disney Channel," Feb. 10, 2009)
http://www.usmagazine.com
(Usmagazine.com, "Demi Lovato: I Was Bullied!" Oct. 1, 2008)
http://variety.com/youthimpactreport
(Variety, "Youth Impact Report," Oct. 3, 2008)

ADDRESS

Demi Lovato
Hollywood Records, Inc.
500 South Buena Vista Street
Burbank, CA 91521

WORLD WIDE WEB SITES

http://www.demilovato.com
http://tv.disney.go.com/disneychannel/originalmovies/camprock
http://tv.disney.go.com/disneychannel/sonnywithachance
http://tv.disney.go.com/disneychannel/originalmovies/princessprotection
program

Michelle Obama 1964-

American Lawyer and Administrator
First Lady of the United States

BIRTH

Michelle Obama was born Michelle LaVaughan Robinson on January 17, 1964, in Chicago, Illinois. She was the second child of Fraser Robinson III, a Chicago city pump operator, and Marian (Shields) Robinson, a homemaker and secretary. Her older brother, Craig Robinson, is her only sibling; he gave up a high-paying career as an investment banker to start a new career as a basketball coach. In 2008 he became head coach of the Oregon State University Beavers.

YOUTH

Obama grew up on the South Side of Chicago, where her family shared the top floor of her great-aunt's bungalow. They didn't have a lot of money, but they made the most of what they had: the family used paneling to split their apartment's living room into separate bedrooms for Michelle and her brother Craig. Obama learned the value of hard work from the example of her parents. Her mother stayed home with the kids until they entered high school, then took a job as a secretary. Fraser Robinson had been diagnosed with multiple sclerosis, a disease that attacks the nerves, before he was even 30 years old. Nevertheless, he went to work every day, even if he had to get up earlier or use a walker to get there on time. Inspired by her parents, young Michelle learned to read before kindergarten, studied hard in school, and skipped the second grade. In sixth grade she took science classes at a local college, hoping she might become a pediatrician some day. She spent many hours practicing the piano and writing stories, but she described herself as "just a typical South Side little black girl. Not a whole lot of money. Going to the circus once a year was a big deal. Getting pizza on Friday was a treat. Summers were long and fun."

> **Obama described herself as "just a typical South Side little black girl. Not a whole lot of money. Going to the circus once a year was a big deal. Getting pizza on Friday was a treat. Summers were long and fun."**

Obama attended Chicago public schools and earned a place into the Whitney M. Young Magnet School for gifted and talented students. She had to travel three hours by bus and train each day, but she was determined to make the most of the opportunity. She was class treasurer and participated in choir, talent shows, and school plays. Although she was athletic and enjoyed competing against her brother, she avoided organized sports because she wanted to avoid the stereotypes that can come with being a tall woman (she is 5'11"). She studied hard, earned all A's, and won a place in the National Honor Society. When her brother earned a basketball scholarship to an Ivy League university, she told herself she could succeed there too. After all, she remembered, "My mother always taught me to work hard to achieve my dreams and to never let anyone tell me that I couldn't do something."

EDUCATION

Obama graduated from Whitney M. Young Magnet School in 1981 and followed her brother Craig to Princeton University, a prestigious Ivy League school in New Jersey. At a school where less than one percent of the students were African American, she sometimes felt like an outsider—her freshman roommate's mother even requested that her daughter be moved. Obama got involved with the Third World Center, an academic and cultural group that supported minority students, and ran a day care they sponsored that included afterschool tutoring. She majored in sociology with a minor in African-American studies and produced a senior thesis examining how the Princeton experience had affected black graduates. She earned her Bachelor of Arts (BA) degree cum laude with departmental honors in 1985. She decided to attend law school and earned a spot at Harvard Law School, another Ivy League institution. There she worked in the Harvard Legal Aid Bureau, assisting low-income tenants with housing cases. She earned her Juris Doctor or Doctor of Law (JD) degree in 1988.

CAREER HIGHLIGHTS

Beginning Her Career in Law

After graduating from Harvard in 1988, Obama took a job with the prestigious Chicago law firm of Sidley & Austin. She served as an associate attorney and specialized in copyright and trademark cases, disputes over who owns rights to ideas. She didn't find the work very interesting, she later noted. "I didn't see a whole lot of people who were just thrilled to be there. I met people who thought this was a good life. But were people waking up just bounding out of bed to get to work? No." Still, with many student loans to pay off, her job at the law firm provided a good paycheck. As she later admitted, "the idea of making more money than both your parents combined ever made is one you don't walk away from."

At Sidley & Austin she first met Barack Obama, when she was assigned to advise him during his summer internship there in 1988. At first, she resisted his invitations to go out, thinking it wouldn't be appropriate because of their work relationship. Besides, "I was more focused on my plan," she said. "I had made this proclamation to my mother the summer I met Barack, 'I'm not worrying about dating … I'm going to focus on me.'" His persistence, and her co-workers' reassurance that they did not disapprove, eventually led to their first date. Michelle soon realized that, although they had grown up in very different environments, she and Barack shared many of the same values: hard work, respect for others, and a commitment to telling the truth. One day she was watching him speak to a group of

Michelle and Barack Obama on their wedding day, October 1992.

church women. "He was able to articulate a vision that resonated with people, that was real," she remembered. "And right then and there, I decided this guy was special. The authenticity you see is real, and that's why I fell in love with him." A friendly game of one-on-one basketball with her brother secured her family's approval, and they eventually got engaged.

In 1991, Michelle Obama suffered two losses that caused her to reassess her life. First, her father died unexpectedly of complications from multiple sclerosis. Only a few months later, a close college friend died of cancer at the age of 25. "It made me realize that I could die tomorrow," she recalled. "I had to ask myself, 'Is this how I want to spend my time?' I knew I would never feel a sense of passion or joy about the law." She decided to leave her law firm and take a pay cut to work as a public servant. In 1991 she became an assistant in the office of Chicago Mayor Richard M. Daley. "I needed to consider what I really cared about, which was work that had a community-based feel, using my education to benefit others," she said. It meant "a temporary financial setback, but in the end, when you're living your dream, the economic stability comes."

Obama decided to leave the law firm to work in public service. "I needed to consider what I really cared about, which was work that had a community-based feel, using my education to benefit others," she said. It meant "a temporary financial setback, but in the end, when you're living your dream, the economic stability comes."

Much of Obama's job in the mayor's office involved helping develop programs for the community, especially lower-income residents like the people she grew up with. She contributed to programs intended to decrease infant mortality, provide afterschool activities for kids, and promote immunization through mobile health facilities. In 1992, she became an assistant commissioner of planning and development for the city of Chicago. She earned a reputation as a troubleshooter who could work with different people to resolve problems quickly.

That same year, in 1992, she married Barack Obama. They held their wedding reception at a cultural center that had once excluded African Americans from their facilities. They went on to have two daughters, Malia and Natasha (Sasha).

Working with the Community

At the suggestion of her husband, Michelle Obama changed jobs again in 1993. He was on the board of Public Allies, an AmeriCorps program that

Obama worked in a variety of positions that combined law, administration, community advocacy, and service to others. At the University of Chicago, shown here, she worked as associate dean of student services & director of the university community service center. Credit: University of Chicago.

prepares youth for public service. The program was starting a Chicago chapter, and Barack Obama suggested that his wife serve as executive director. (He left the board after she was hired to avoid any potential conflicts of interest.) It meant another pay cut, but Michelle Obama had become frustrated by the slow pace of city bureaucracy. The new job "sounded risky and just out there," she later said. "But for some reason it spoke to me. This was the first time I said, 'This is what I say I care about. Right here. And I will have to run it.'"

As someone who had grown up on Chicago's South Side but gone on to the Ivy League, Obama had a unique perspective. "We had people who had just graduated high school taking internships alongside people who had just graduated from Harvard," she noted. "I learned that you can go to the best school in the country and still not realize what you can do to help the community." She would later call her job at Public Allies "by far the best thing I've done in my professional career. It was the first thing that was mine, and I was responsible for every aspect of it." After three years of working 60-hour weeks, Obama had established a strong program.

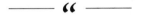

Obama questioned her husband's involvement in politics. "But each and every time I confronted that doubt in my own mind," she recalled, "I started thinking beyond myself.... I started thinking about the type of person that I want to see in politics. And that always turned out to be a guy like Barack."

In 1996 Obama brought her experience working with youth to the University of Chicago, taking a position as associate dean of student services and director of the university community service center. She helped the university develop a community service program that tried to get students involved in the local area. That same year, her husband ran for the Illinois State Senate. Michelle Obama wasn't thrilled with the idea and told her husband, "I married you because you're cute and you're smart, but this is the dumbest thing you could have ever asked me to do." She has said that she was cynical about politics and wondered whether it was really the best use of her husband's time. "But each and every time I confronted that doubt in my own mind," she recalled, "I started thinking beyond myself.... I started thinking about the type of person that I want to see in politics. And that always turned out to be a guy like Barack." He won that election and was re-elected in 1998, the same year their first child was born. In 2000 he made his first bid for national office. He ran in the Democratic primary for a seat in the U.S. House of Representatives, but lost in the primary. He returned to the Illinois Senate in 2002.

Michelle Obama has spoken frequently of challenges she faced as a working mom. "Every other month [since] I've had children I've struggled with the notion of 'Am I being a good parent? Can I stay home? Should I stay home? How do I balance it all?'" she admitted. "I have gone back and forth every year about whether I should work." When interviewing for a job at the University of Chicago Hospitals in 2002, for example, she hadn't been able to find a babysitter for her new baby daughter, so she brought her along in a stroller. Although she wanted to be home for her girls, she enjoyed the sense of independence and self-worth that come from a job well done. "Work is rewarding," she stated. "I love losing myself in a set of problems that have nothing to do with my husband and children. Once you've tasted that, it's hard to walk away."

Still, with her husband often away in the State Senate or campaigning, Obama was left to manage the household and kids by herself much of the time. She felt resentful, until she finally came to terms with the demands of her husband's political career and accepted that help didn't have to come from him. "I spent a lot of time expecting my husband to fix things, but then I came to realize that he was there in the ways he could be," she observed. Instead, she asked herself, "How do I structure my world so that it works for me and I'm not trying to get him to be what I think he should be?" She got help from friends, from neighbors, and especially from her mother. She is not shy about sharing these early difficulties with people. "I think every couple struggles with these issues," she said. "People don't tell you how much kids change things.... If we can talk about it, we can help each other."

Becoming a Political Asset

In 2002, Obama took a job with the University of Chicago Medical Center as executive director of community affairs. The University of Chicago and its affiliated hospitals are considered among the best in the country, but many local residents feel shut out. "I grew up five minutes from the university and never once went on campus," she stated. "All the buildings have their backs to the community. The university didn't think kids like me existed, and I certainly didn't want anything to do with that place." Obama began several programs that reached out to poorer neighborhoods near the hospital. As a result, the number of hospital employees serving in community clinics increased five times, and the number of volunteers coming in from the community multiplied four times. In addition, she also contributed to the hospital's efforts to improve staff diversity, helping to recruit minority doctors to the hospital.

Meanwhile, Barack Obama's political career was taking off. But when he was elected to the U.S. Senate in 2004, the Obamas decided that Michelle and the girls would stay in Chicago. "I have a big village here," she commented at the time, referring to the adage that it takes a village to raise a child. "Unless it was absolutely necessary, we felt it would just be good to stay close to our base. It's proven to be a smart move, and he's come to understand the wisdom of my plan." Because he arranged his schedule to be home Thursday through Sunday, the family often saw him more often than when he was serving and campaigning as a state senator. Later that year Barack Obama began to develop a broader national profile when he gave a keynote speech at the Democratic National Convention that was widely praised. His book *Dreams from My Father* hit the bestseller list, bringing the family extra financial security, and people began talking of a possible presidential run in the future.

In the meantime, Michelle Obama was promoted to vice-president of community and external affairs at the University of Chicago Medical Center in 2005, a promotion that also brought her a six-figure salary. Her new responsibilities included working on a contracting system that would encourage the hiring of more women- and minority-owned businesses. Obama also started a program to get local residents to use health clinics instead of emergency rooms. She felt this was important because, according to medical studies, poor residents who wait to go to the emergency room for medical treatment often become sicker than those who have access to primary care clinics. Obama created mobile units to bring medical services for children into poorer neighborhoods and increased volunteer participation in programs. She earned praise from community leaders for her management style. She didn't just try to make things easier for the hospital, but showed real concern for the public's needs as well. In 2005, she and her family also moved into a $1.6 million home on Chicago's South Side. "I'm in the community where I grew up, where I live, and it feels like it's all coming full circle," she said.

"Every other month [since] I've had children I've struggled with the notion of 'Am I being a good parent? Can I stay home? Should I stay home? How do I balance it all?'" Obama acknowledged. "I have gone back and forth every year about whether I should work." But she also said that "Work is rewarding. I love losing myself in a set of problems that have nothing to do with my husband and children. Once you've tasted that, it's hard to walk away."

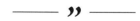

At the same time, Barack Obama was getting more political support for a possible presidential run. In 2006 he published another bestselling book, *The Audacity of Hope,* and the following year he announced his candidacy to become president. By now he had earned his wife's full support. "Barack is special, and I'm willing to share him…. I'm willing to share the girls," she said. "If we can have better schools and health care and help moms who are struggling and get back on track internationally, then all this? Big deal. I can handle it."

MALIA AND SASHA OBAMA

Malia Obama was born on July 4, 1998, in Chicago, Illinois. She is the more serious of the Obama girls; her mom calls her "focused." She attends Sidwell Friends School and plays soccer and tennis. She also has taken dance, drama, and piano lessons. She enjoys photography and could be seen taking pictures during the Inauguration. She lists ice cream as her favorite food, and enjoyed reading the Harry Potter series together with her dad. She has some allergies, which is why her family was careful in choosing a pet dog for the family. Malia says she would like to become an actress when she grows up, but she plans to get a good education in case it doesn't work out.

Natasha Obama was born on June 10, 2001, in Chicago, Illinois. She's known as Sasha. During the 2008 campaign, she often could be seen waving to crowds; her mom calls her a ham. She attends Sidwell Friends School and joined the basketball team so she could share the sport with her father. She has also taken gymnastics, tap dance, tennis, and piano lessons. Sasha is a big fan of the Jonas Brothers and Hannah Montana, and she would like to be a singer or dancer when she grows up.

Until their father was elected president, the Obama girls spent most of their time in Chicago, going to school and spending time with friends. When school was out, they might accompany their parents on a campaign trip; otherwise, they kept to their daily routine with their mother or grandmother. They had to leave all their friends and activities behind when the Obamas moved from Chicago to Washington DC. They moved into the White House on January 21, 2009, the day their father was inaugurated. They had a sleepover that night, with a scavenger hunt to help introduce them to their new home. As a bonus, their favorite band, the Jonas Brothers, stopped by for a visit.

Living in the White House has many other benefits. It has its own swimming pool, bowling alley, tennis and basketball courts, and movie theater. The girls got to redecorate their rooms, and they made room for Bo, the new dog they were promised during the campaign. Best of all, because they now live in the same building as their dad's office, they get to have dinner together as a family every night. Despite all these bonuses, the Obama girls still have to do chores. They set and clear the dinner table, make their own beds, do homework, practice the piano, and clean up their play areas. Bedtime is at 8:30, unless they want an extra half hour to read, and they have to get themselves up and ready for school. As their mom explained: "I want the kids to be treated like children, not little princesses."

As the campaign got underway, Michelle Obama reduced her work hours at the University of Chicago to help her husband campaign. She made speaking appearances by herself—usually without notes—and often drew crowds in the thousands. Although she traveled all over the country, she always tried to be home for her daughters' bedtime. "You've got to make trade-offs in life," she said. "I'm okay with that. I've come to realize I am sacrificing one set of things in my life for something else potentially really positive." In the end, she noted, "the little sacrifice we have to make is nothing compared to the possibility of what we could do if this catches on." Of course, she added, she couldn't have done any of it without the help of her mother, who retired from her secretarial job to watch the two girls.

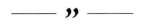

"In our generation, we were just taught that if you know who you are, then what somebody calls you is just so irrelevant.... If I wilted every time someone in my life mischaracterized me or called me a bad name, I would have never finished Princeton, would have never gone to Harvard, and wouldn't be sitting here with [Barack Obama]," she said. "My view on this stuff is I'm just trying to be myself, trying to be as authentic as I can be," she said. "I can't pretend to be somebody else."

The Road to the White House

Michelle Obama's style on the campaign trail was forthright, down-to-earth, and sometimes controversial. In February 2008, she was speaking of the number of new voters getting involved in the political process when she said, "For the first time in my adult life, I am proud of my country." She said her words were taken out of context—she had always been proud of America, but not of a political system that once denied rights to some citizens. But critics still questioned her patriotism and tried to stereotype her as an angry black woman. Obama didn't let the criticism bother her, a lesson she says she learned as a girl. "In our generation, we were just taught that if you know who you are, then what somebody calls you is just so irrelevant.... If I wilted every time someone in my life mischaracterized me or called me a bad name, I would have never finished Princeton, would have never gone to Harvard, and wouldn't be sitting here with [Barack Obama]." She kept going on the campaign trail, making appearances on national television and dealing with any con-

President Barack Obama and First Lady Michelle Obama wave to the crowd as they make their way down Pennsylvania Avenue during the 2009 presidential inaugural parade in Washington DC, January 2009.

———— " ————

"The truth is, I'm not supposed to be here, standing here," Obama said. "I'm a statistical oddity. Black girl, brought up on the South Side of Chicago. Was I supposed to go to Princeton? No.... They said maybe Harvard Law was too much for me to reach for. But I went, I did fine...."

———— " ————

troversy head-on. "My view on this stuff is I'm just trying to be myself, trying to be as authentic as I can be," she said. "I can't pretend to be somebody else." Many people were charmed by her style and confidence, and as the public got to know her better, her approval ratings went up.

In August 2008, Michelle Obama spoke at the Democratic National Convention, where her husband would be officially nominated as the Democratic candidate for president. She gave a heartfelt speech, sharing the story of her life and her belief "that each of us—no matter what our age or background or walk of life— each of us has something to contribute to the life of this nation." On November 4, 2008, Barack Obama was elected president, becoming the first African American to achieve the office. For Michelle Obama, it wasn't just her husband's historic victory that made the campaign worthwhile. "It has been a blessing for us to have this opportunity to spend this year traveling the country," she noted. "We've been in almost every state in this nation—in people's homes, in their kitchens, in their community centers—and just having the opportunity to be reminded of how decent the American people are and how our values are so closely linked, that gives me hope."

As the Obamas got ready to move into the White House, Michelle Obama said that her primary focus was on making the transition easy for her daughters. She resigned her position at the University of Chicago Medical Center and invited her mother, Marian Robinson, to join them in Washington. She started looking for new schools for the girls in Washington. She was eager to make a home for her family in the White House, but she also wanted to make it more open to the public. "We feel privileged, and we feel a responsibility to make it feel like the people's house," she said. "We have the good fortune to sleep here, but this house belongs to America."

First Lady of the United States

Barack Obama was sworn in as the 44th president in January 2009. As he became president, Michelle Obama became first lady. This is a position with no set duties; each president's wife has molded the role to fit her concerns. Traditionally, first ladies have one or two issues they plan to promote, and Obama said she wanted to bring attention to work-family issues (especially for military families) and increasing public service among young people.

The new First Lady quickly made good on her promises to begin working for the American people. She spent time volunteering, putting together care packages for members of the military. She made visits to cabinet-level agencies to familiarize herself with Washington politics and say thank you. She also dropped in on local schools, church groups, and community centers, including some time volunteering at a soup kitchen. "[Washington DC] is our community now," she said. "It's our home." As for opening the White House, she hosted tours of the White House kitchens for local cuisine students, sponsored a "bring your child to work" day, and offered a "girls' night in" with movies for secretaries and staff alike. She invited the media to watch as she established an organic kitchen garden, complete with beehive, and had a play set installed on the White House lawn. She had come into the White House with the highest favorability ratings of any incoming first lady since 1980, at 46%; after three months, her approval ratings were up to 76%, including 60% of Republicans.

The first lady has also found a new role as fashion icon, which she has found surprising. Obama is tall and fit and enjoys looking her best, but she didn't expect people to pay that much attention to her clothing. While she does enjoy occasional designer outfits, her fashion choices are often practical, and many of her outfits have come from retail chains like J. Crew. "First and foremost, I wear what I love," she explained. "That's what women have to focus on: what makes them happy and what makes them feel comfortable and beautiful. If I can have any impact, I want women to feel good about themselves and have fun with fashion." She charmed the European press during a spring 2009 visit, although that may have had less to do with her fashion sense and more with the genuine warmth and emotion she displayed when talking with underprivileged students in London.

"I know that all I can do is be the best me that I can. And live life with some gusto. Giving back is a big part of that. How am I going to share this experience with the American people? I'm always thinking about that."

The first lady can take on a lot of different roles, as shown here: working with children to create a White House garden; speaking to elected leaders and others about important issues; and advocating for education while visiting a local bilingual school.

For Michelle Obama, life in the White House has been more than she ever dreamed. Best of all, she said, "We have dinner as a family together every night, and Barack, when he's not traveling, tucks the girls in. We haven't had that kind of time together for [years], so that explains a lot [of] why we all feel so good in this space." She is happy to be a partner in her husband's political career, and he supports her in return. "He's my biggest cheerleader, as a mother, as a wife and as a career person," she said. "He is always telling me how great I'm doing. That helps keep you going when you realize that you have someone who appreciates all the hard work that you are doing." As for finding her new role challenging, she said, "I have very full days. When we're done, I can structure a more formal career if that's where I choose to go."

Right now, Obama is satisfied to serve the country as a first lady and as a role model. "The truth is, I'm not supposed to be here, standing here," she said. "I'm a statistical oddity. Black girl, brought up on the South Side of Chicago. Was I supposed to go to Princeton? No.... They said maybe Harvard Law was too much for me to reach for. But I went, I did fine." In the end, she remarked, "I know that all I can do is be the best me that I can. And live life with some gusto. Giving back is a big part of that. How am I going to share this experience with the American people? I'm always thinking about that."

MARRIAGE AND FAMILY

Robinson married Barack Obama on October 18, 1992. Their first daughter, Malia Ann, was born July 4, 1998; their second daughter, Natasha (nicknamed Sasha), was born on June 10, 2001. After moving into the White House in 2009, the family added a pet, a Portuguese water dog called Bo, to the family. They still maintain a home in Chicago's Hyde Park neighborhood and plan to return there after President's Obama's time in office is over.

HOBBIES AND OTHER INTERESTS

As a working mom, Obama has little free time to indulge in hobbies. She makes room in her schedule to work out at least four times a week; she says that fitness "has become even more important as I've had children, because I'm also thinking about how I'm modeling health to my daughters." Otherwise, she enjoys spending time with her family and friends, especially watching movies and playing board games together.

HONORS AND AWARDS

Woman of the Year (*Essence magazine*): 2008

Books

Brophy, David Bergen. *Michelle Obama: Meet the First Lady,* 2009 (young adult)
Colbert, David. *Michelle Obama: An American Story,* 2009 (young adult)

Periodicals

Chicago Magazine, Feb. 2009, p.50
Chicago Sun-Times, Sep. 1, 2004; Apr. 22, 2007; July 9, 2008
Chicago Tribune, Feb. 26, 2009
Current Biography Yearbook, 2008
Daily Princetonian, Dec. 7, 2005
Ebony, Mar. 2006, p.58; Feb. 2007, p.52; Sep. 2008, p.72
Essence, Sep. 2007, p.200; Sep. 2008, p.150; Jan. 2009
Good Housekeeping, Nov. 2008, p.144
Maclean's, Apr. 20, 2009, p.24
People, June 18, 2007, p.118; July 23, 2008; Aug. 4, 2008, p.50; Feb. 2, 2009, p.69; Mar. 9, 2009, p.112
New York, Mar. 23, 2009, p.26
New Yorker, May 31, 2004; Mar. 10, 2008, p.88
New York Times, Aug. 26, 2007, p.A1; Jan. 20, 2009, p.A1; Feb. 8. 2009, p.A18
Newsweek, Jan. 29. 2007, p.40; Feb. 25, 2008, p.26
O, the Oprah Magazine, Sep. 2005, p.22; Nov. 2007, p.286; Apr. 2009, p.140
USA Today, July 5, 2008
U.S. News & World Report, Feb. 11, 2008, p. 14
Us Weekly, Nov. 24, 2008, p.46
Vogue, Sep. 2007, p.774; Mar. 2009, p.428
Washington Post, May 11, 2007, p.A1

Online Articles

http://abcnews.go.com/GMA/Vote2008/story?id=5643969&page=1
   (ABC News, "Who Is Michelle Obama," Aug. 25, 2008)
http://www.ebonyjet.com/ebony/articles/index.aspx?id=8650
   (Ebony, "The Real Michelle Obama," Aug. 6, 2008)
http://www.essence.com/news_entertainment/news/articles/michelleobama
   besidebarack
   (Essence, "Michelle Obama, Beside Barack," Nov. 5, 2008)
http://topics.nytimes.com/top/reference/timestopics/people/o/michelle_
   obama/index.html
   (New York Times, "Times Topics," multiple articles, various dates)
http://topics.newsweek.com/people/politics/obama-administration/
   michelle-obama.htm
   (Newsweek, "Michelle Obama," multiple articles, various dates)

http://www.pbs.org/newshour/bb/politics/jan-june09/firstlady_03-12.html
(PBS, Michelle Obama Works to Define Agenda as First Lady," Mar. 21, 2009)
http://www.time.com/time/politics/article/0,8599,1900067,00.html
(Time, "The Meaning of Michelle," May 21, 2009)

ADDRESS

Michelle Obama
The White House
1600 Pennsylvania Ave. NW
Washington, D.C. 20500

WORLD WIDE WEB SITES

http://www.whitehouse.gov
http://www.barackobama.com/about/michelle_obama

Robert Pattinson 1986-

British Actor
Star of *Harry Potter and the Goblet of Fire* and *The
Twilight Saga* Films

BIRTH

Robert Thomas Pattinson was born on May 13, 1986, in London, England. He was the third and youngest child of Richard
Pattinson, a vintage car salesman, and Clare Pattinson, who
worked for a modeling agency. He grew up with two older sisters, Victoria and Elizabeth (Lizzy).

YOUTH

Pattinson had a fairly traditional childhood growing up in the southwest London suburb of Barnes. He attended a private boys' school nearby, the Tower House School, where he occasionally performed in school plays. He wasn't a terrific student, and his report cards showed it. "They were always pretty bad—I never ever did my homework," he admitted. "I always turned up for lessons, as I liked my teachers, but my report said I didn't try very hard." At age 12, he moved to a mixed private school, the Harrodian School, which emphasized helping students reach their potential, both academically and socially. Pattinson enjoyed his new school, especially having girls as classmates. "I became cool and discovered hair gel," he recalled. At the same time he began modeling. He modeled for about three years, when he grew up and "stopped looking like a girl," as he put it.

> *Pattinson got involved with acting mostly because he hoped to meet girls. "My dad spotted a bunch of girls in a café and they were all really excited, so he asked them where they'd been," he recalled. "When they said that they'd been to drama classes, he reckoned I should get myself down there!"*

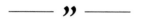

Pattinson had many interests as a teenager. He enjoyed sports like soccer, snowboarding, and skiing, and he explored music by playing piano and guitar. But he still wasn't a big success at school, either academically or socially. "I wasn't with the cool gang, or the uncool ones," he recalled. "I was transitional, in between." In fact, he got involved with acting mostly because he hoped to meet girls. "My dad spotted a bunch of girls in a café and they were all really excited, so he asked them where they'd been," Pattinson recalled. "When they said that they'd been to drama classes, he reckoned I should get myself down there!" He began by working backstage and eventually landed a leading role.

EDUCATION

In England, students complete secondary school at the age of 16. For those going to university, they take a couple of years of additional classes that prepare them for Advanced-Level exams, called A-Levels, in different subjects. After Pattinson completed secondary school at the Harrodian School, he wanted to continue his studies. Because he had been focusing more on acting than school, his father told him he would have to pay his own way; if he scored well on his exams, his father would reimburse him for the tuition. Pattinson used his fees from acting and modeling to continue A-Level studies at Harrodian, and he finished three A-Level exams. His scores weren't terrific, and he later revealed that he never really intended to go to college.

CAREER HIGHLIGHTS

Becoming an Actor

Pattinson got his start as an actor when he was still in high school. When he was 15 he joined the Barnes Theatre Company (BTC), a local theater group that produced a couple of stage productions each year. After working backstage for one production, he auditioned for a role in *Guys and Dolls,* an award-winning musical from 1950. He only got a small part, but he gave it his best, something his fellow actors noticed. "They respected me for doing it and gave me the lead in Thornton Wilder's *Our Town,*" he said. The role of George Gibbs in *Our Town* is challenging, portraying a teenager who falls in love, grows up and marries, and then faces the death of his wife. Pattinson's performance in the role earned him a professional agent.

Pattinson continued to appear in local stage productions, including the classic Cole Porter musical *Anything Goes,* the Shakespearean tragedy *Macbeth,* and the drama *Tess of the D'Urbervilles,* based on the 19th-century novel by Thomas Hardy. Pattinson played the villainous role of Alec, who ruins a young girl and forces her to become his mistress.

By the time he was 17, Pattinson had begun earning small parts in films and television shows He earned a larger part in the 2004 European TV miniseries *Ring of the Nibelungs.* (The show was later broadcast in the United States on the SciFi Channel as *Dark Kingdom: The Dragon King.*) In this adaptation of a Germanic myth, Pattinson played a prince whose family is ensnared in the magical adventures of the dragon slayer Siegfried. The four-hour series was filmed entirely in South Africa, giving the young actor experience living on his own and working on a production with special effects. As he remembered, "I was there for three months in an apartment at just 17! So I came back really confident."

Winning a Role in the *Harry Potter* Films

Pattinson's confidence helped for his next audition, for the next installment of the blockbuster film franchise based on the *Harry Potter* books by J.K. Rowling. (For more information on Rowling, see *Biography Today,* Jan.

Pattinson as Cedric Diggory in scenes from Harry Potter and the Goblet of Fire: *conferring with his competitor, Harry; battling through the maze; and approaching the goblet of fire.*

2008.) Although the books had sold millions of copies around the world, Pattinson hadn't read any of them before he learned of the opportunity to audition for the fourth film, *Harry Potter and the Goblet of Fire.* He was up for the part of Cedric Diggory, an older student who competes against Harry in a magical tournament between wizarding schools. Pattinson quickly read the book to give himself an idea of the character, then had an initial audition for director Mike Newell before heading to South Africa to film *Ring of the Nibelungs.* The day after he returned, he was called back for a second audition. Soon after he got the news: he had won a key role in what would be the biggest movie of 2005.

In working on *Harry Potter and the Goblet of Fire,* Pattinson was joining a cast that had already worked on three films together. But after a few weeks of acting exercises with the other young actors, he felt like just another one of the gang. "I didn't notice the transition to being accepted, but they are all really nice people," he recalled. "It seems like it should have been daunting but it wasn't." More intimidating was the thought of working with such distinguished British actors as Sir Michael Gambon (Dumbledore), Dame Maggie Smith (Professor McGonagall), and Warwick Davis (Professor Flitwick), who starred in one of Pattinson's favorite films, the 1988 fantasy *Willow.* It inspired Pattinson to try his best. "I put quite a lot of work into it in the beginning," he recalled. "So I ignored all my nerves by sitting and looking at the script or reading the book 10 times." His preparations also included fitness and scuba training for some of the action scenes, as well as dance lessons for the ballroom scene.

> *The character of Cedric Diggory—school prefect, Quidditch captain, and Hogwarts' champion for the Triwizard Tournament—was appealing to Pattinson. "He's not really a complete cliché of the good kid in school. He's just quiet," he observed. "He is actually just a genuinely good person, but he doesn't make a big deal about it or anything. I can kind of relate to that."*

The character of Cedric Diggory—school prefect, Quidditch captain, and Hogwarts' champion for the Triwizard Tournament—was appealing to Pattinson. "He's not really a complete cliché of the good kid in school. He's just quiet," he observed. "He is actually just a genuinely good person, but he doesn't make a big deal about it or anything. I can kind of relate to that." Although he might have looked the part, Pattinson didn't feel he

Pattinson and Kristen Stewart in a scene from Twilight.

was like his character at all. "I was never a leader, and the idea of my ever being made head boy would have been a complete joke," he acknowledged. "I wasn't involved in much at school, and I was never picked for any of the teams." Nevertheless, he enjoyed filming the various action scenes, which included many special effects and moving around huge sets. "It was amazing. It was a very different thing to anything I've ever experienced," he said at the time.

Harry Potter and the Goblet of Fire was a big hit at the box office, winning the approval of the series' many fans. Although it was the first *Harry Potter* film to be rated PG-13, it had the best opening weekend of any of the films to date, and it had the biggest worldwide receipts at the box office for 2005. In addition to his role in *Goblet of Fire,* Pattinson appeared in flashback in the fifth film, *Harry Potter and the Order of the Phoenix* (2007).

Trying New Roles

After completing his high-profile role in *Goblet of Fire,* Pattinson could have looked for similar good-guy roles. Instead he pursued a role on the London stage as a troubled youth, then won roles in a couple of British TV productions. In the 2006 mystery *The Haunted Airman,* based on the novel by Dennis Wheatley, he played a former Royal Air Force pilot who was wounded during World War II. Confined to a wheelchair, the pilot begins suffering hallucinations and nightmares, but it is unclear whether he is losing his mind or there is a sinister plot behind his decline. Pattinson had a smaller role in the 2007 family drama, *The Bad Mother's Handbook.* It follows the relationships between a grandmother, mother, and daughter; Pattinson played a nerdy friend of the daughter.

Pattinson was beginning to wonder whether he should keep acting when he decided to move to Los Angeles and try auditioning for some American roles. His first task was mastering the accent. That wasn't hard, he said, since "I grew up watching American movies and stuff, so I've learned how to 'act' from American films." He soon got an audition for an adaptation of another popular book: the vampire romance *Twilight,* written by Stephenie Meyer. *Twilight* is the first in a series of books that now includes *New Moon, Eclipse,* and *Breaking Dawn.*

When *Twilight* film director Catherine Hardwicke saw Pattinson's audition, she was impressed by his chemistry with costar Kristen Stewart, as well as his otherworldly looks, and she cast him in the lead role of Edward. Thousands of fans protested, believing the part should be played by someone more famous and more handsome.

The concept of playing a "pretty boy" has been a struggle for Pattinson. "I literally have to be filmed from the right angle or I look deformed. I'm not just one of those guys you can shoot from any angle and they look perfect."

After author Stephenie Meyer gave him her approval, calling him someone "who can look both dangerous and beautiful at the same time," the fans came around. "The funny thing is I've been trying to get pretty boy roles for the last four years and nobody cast me," Pattinson commented. "It's like the world has changed its mind this year." The concept of playing a "pretty boy" has been a struggle for Pattinson. "I literally have to be filmed from the right angle or I look deformed. I'm not just one of those guys you can shoot from any angle and they look perfect."

Appearing in *Twilight*

Pattinson worked hard to prepare for the role of Edward, reflecting on the character's personality, actions, and feelings. He headed to Oregon, where it was filmed, ahead of the rest of the cast. There he spent a lot of time alone, reading the script and books and avoiding people. "Edward would be so bored with any kind of human interaction," he explained. "He would not feel like he was part of the human world." The actor thought about why a vampire over 100 years old would still be in high school. "You think he'd stay in college, or be a street kid," the actor mused. "It'd be way cooler. But I think the whole concept of it is: He's like an addict. I think he wants to make his life really, really, really boring." Although in the book Edward is described as almost perfect, both in looks and personality, "I just kind of ignored it," Pattinson said. "I just tried to concentrate on his flaws." His approach was to play Edward almost as a manic-depressive. "I tried to play it, as much as possible, like a 17-year-old boy who had this purgatory inflicted on him." His goal was to make Edward as real a character as possible. "I never saw it as a vampire," he remarked. "I saw it as a guy with something in him that makes him terrified of commitment."

> Pattinson worked hard to prepare for the role of Edward. "I tried to play it, as much as possible, like a 17-year-old boy who had this purgatory inflicted on him." His goal was to make Edward as real a character as possible. "I never saw it as a vampire," he remarked. "I saw it as a guy with something in him that makes him terrified of commitment."

The story in *Twilight* focuses on the growing—and dangerous—love between Bella Swan, an ordinary human teenager, and Edward Cullen, a vampire. Bella moves to a new town to live with her father, the local sheriff. On her first day of school, she meets her new lab partner, Edward. He has sworn not to feed off humans, but he finds Bella's scent intoxicating. She falls in love with him, which becomes especially dangerous when other vampires show up in town. As Pattinson sees it, "Edward is essentially the hero of this story but violently denies that he is the hero.... He refuses to accept Bella's love for him but at the same time can't help but just kind of need it."

In addition to acting in the film, Pattinson contributed some songs as well. Someone gave director Hardwicke a recording of his songs, and she used two of them in the film without telling him about it. "It was like [the song] was supposed to be there.... It's this little song with acoustic guitar. I'm singing it, maybe that makes it different, but it's kind of overwhelming." His

Pattinson (right) with Taylor Lautner and Kristen Stewart at the 2009 MTV Awards, where the movie Twilight *and the cast took home several awards.*

song "Never Think," co-written with a friend, appeared on the film's official soundtrack, which hit No. 1 on Billboard's Top 200 Album Chart and was certified platinum with over one million copies sold. Although he loves music, Pattinson hasn't recorded anything seriously, preferring to play small gigs in bars with friends. "I really didn't want it to look like I was trying to cash in.... I'm not going to be doing any music videos or anything. Music is my backup plan if acting fails. I don't want to put all my eggs in one basket."

Twilight debuted in November 2008 and earned almost $70 million in its first weekend alone. While that may have surprised those unfamiliar with the books, it certainly didn't surprise devoted *Twilight* fans, who saw the film multiple times. This story of forbidden love eventually led to $191 million in sales at the box office in the U.S. alone, making *Twilight* the top vampire movie of all time. According to many critics, Pattinson was a big reason for the movie's success. "Pattinson walks away with every scene he's in," a London *Times* online reporter wrote, while *Entertainment Weekly* critic Owen Gleiberman noted that "Pattinson has a look so broodingly unearthly it's no wonder he doesn't sprout fangs. His creepy bedroom stare is a special effect all its own." In addition, the movie and its cast won a host of awards at the MTV movie awards, including best movie; best male breakthrough performance for Pattinson; best female performance for Kristen Stewart; best kiss for Pattinson and Stewart; and best fight for Pattinson and Cam Gigandet.

Following the success of *Twilight,* the movie studio was eager to film the sequels. *New Moon* is currently scheduled to be released in November 2009, followed by *Eclipse* in June 2010. Pattinson will reprise the role of Edward in both films.

Expanding His Acting Range

It seems likely that Pattinson has a long career as an actor ahead of him. His role in *Twilight* brought him lots of attention, with crowds of over 5,000 coming to some of his public appearances. The readers of the London *Times* Online voted him "British Star of Tomorrow." Low-budget, independent movies that he filmed before *Twilight* suddenly got more attention, and they demonstrated Pattinson could play a wide range of characters. He played one such character, Art, in the 2008 film *How to Be.* Art is a failed musician whose girlfriend kicks him out, forcing him to move back home with his parents. He then uses an inheritance to hire a self-help guru as his personal life-coach. The film appeared at several festivals in 2008 and earned Pattinson a Best Actor Award from the Strasbourg (France) International Film Festival.

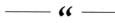

Pattinson admits to being somewhat shy, especially when it comes to talking about himself, and he would prefer not to give interviews. "I just say the first thing that comes into my head out of nervousness."

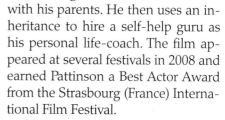

Pattinson took a completely different role in *Little Ashes,* which also appeared at film festivals in 2008 and was released in theaters in 2009, after his success in *Twilight.* In this biography, he plays the Spanish painter Salvador Dalí, best known for surrealist landscapes that often featured melting clocks, eggs, ants, and spindly figures. The role was challenging and complex, playing the artist as a youth in the early 1920s, when he became involved with two other future artistic giants, poet Federico García Lorca and filmmaker Luis Buñuel. "I didn't want to get stuck in pretty, public school roles, or I knew I'd end up as some sort of caricature," Pattinson said. "Playing Dalí has been a complete turning point for me…. He was the most bizarre, complex man, but in the end I felt I could relate to him. He was basically incredibly shy."

Pattinson in a scene from How to Be.

Pattinson's success in *Twilight* has brought him fame and fortune—including a reported $10 million a picture for the sequels. But he dislikes all the media attention he has been getting. "It's boring! I'm thinking about my career in long terms, rather than just trying to milk one thing for whatever it's worth." He also admits to being somewhat shy, especially when it comes to talking about himself, and he would prefer not to give interviews. "I just say the first thing that comes into my head out of nervousness."

Pattinson has said that his future might involve writing and producing, both films and music. His goal is to create work that is creatively fulfilling, in whatever field. "I'm not massively concerned about doing lots of acting jobs," he remarked. "If it all just went, right now, I'd be like, 'All right. I don't really care.' That's probably a stupid thing to say. But I don't, really. I think it'd be much worse to do a load of stuff that's really bad. Because then you can't go into another career. If you've made an idiot out of yourself, you're never going to be taken seriously, as a lawyer or something, if you're, like, a joke actor. The only thing I want from anything is to not be embarrassed." As for his success, he keeps it all in perspective. "It's hard for [my parents] because they want to be proud of me, but I keep reminding them that it's all luck. Luck is what got me here, nothing else."

HOME AND FAMILY

Pattinson spends time in both London and Los Angeles. For a time he shared an apartment with a friend in London's Soho neighborhood, but since his success in *Twilight* he has begun renting his own place in Los Angeles. "Really, I'm a bit of a loner and not that good with dealing with loads of people," he has said. "Most of the time, I feel that going out is a complete waste of time. I'd rather stay in and create something than go out and talk."

HOBBIES AND OTHER INTERESTS

Besides playing and listening to music, Pattinson spends his free time playing cards and darts. He also enjoys writing in a journal. When at home in London, he loves to spend time with his dog, Patty, a white West Highland terrier.

MOVIE AND TELEVISION CREDITS

Ring of the Nibelungs, 2004 (European TV; aired in the U.S. as Dark Kingdom: The Dragon King, 2006)
Harry Potter and the Goblet of Fire, 2005
The Haunted Airman, 2006 (British TV)
Harry Potter and the Order of the Phoenix, 2007
The Bad Mother's Handbook, 2007 (British TV)
How to Be, 2008
The Summer House, 2008 (short film)
Twilight, 2008
Little Ashes, 2009

HONORS AND AWARDS

Festival Prize for Best Actor (Strasbourg International Film Festival): 2008, for *How to Be*
New Hollywood Award (Hollywood Film Festival): 2008
MTV Movie Awards: 2009 (three awards), for *Twilight*, for Best Male Breakthrough Performance, Best Kiss (with Kristen Stewart), and Best Fight (with Cam Gigandet)

FURTHER READING

Books

Adams, Isabelle. *Robert Pattinson: Eternally Yours*, 2008

Periodicals

Boston Globe, Nov. 16, 2008, p.N9
Chicago Tribune, Nov. 14, 2008
Daily Mail (London), Dec. 5, 2008, p.45

Daily Telegraph (London), Dec. 5, 2008, p.32
Entertainment Weekly, Nov. 14, 2008, p.24; Nov. 28, 2008, p.58
GQ, Apr. 2009, p.102
Los Angeles Times, Nov. 2, 2008, p.E5
Maclean's, Dec. 8, 2008, p.52
New York Times, Nov. 16, 2008, p.L4
USA Today, Nov. 20, 2008, p.D1; Nov. 21, 2008, p.E4

Online Articles

http://women.timesonline.co.uk
   (London Times, "Fancy Man: Robert Pattinson," Dec. 14, 2008)
http://latimesblogs.latimes.com
   (Los Angeles Times, "Robert Pattinson on his *Twilight* Songs," Oct. 9, 2008)
http://www.mtv.com/movies
   (MTV, "What's in Store for Robert Pattinson's Post-*Twilight* Future?"
   Feb. 25, 2009)

ADDRESS

Robert Pattinson
Summit Entertainment
1630 Stewart Street
Suite 120
Santa Monica, CA 90404

WORLD WIDE WEB SITES

http://www.twilightthemovie.com
http://www.stepheniemeyer.com

Gloria Gilbert Stoga 1955?-

American Dog Training Program Organizer
Founder and President of Puppies Behind Bars

MAJOR ACCOMPLISHMENTS

Gloria Gilbert Stoga is the founder and president of Puppies Behind Bars. This nonprofit organization uses prison inmate volunteers to raise and train guide dogs for the blind, service dogs for the disabled, and explosive-detection dogs for law enforcement. As of 2009, it had produced over 335 working dogs.

The first seed of this innovative program took root in 1990, when Stoga and her husband adopted a Labrador retriever named Arrow. Arrow had participated in a program to train guide dogs for the blind, but he was released for medical reasons. When she adopted Arrow, Stoga learned about all the time, money, and effort that went into training dogs like him. She discovered that guide dogs and service dogs spend their early lives with specially trained puppy raisers. These individuals care for the dogs for 16 months. During this time, the puppy raisers teach the dogs basic obedience skills, help them become comfortable in different situations, and help them to gain confidence. Dogs that excel in this phase go on to receive further training at guide dog schools.

———— " ————

Stoga believed Puppies behind Bars could benefit the disabled and the inmates alike. "It made so much sense," she thought, "to have people who can give love, who have a lot of time, who need to be rehabilitated, and put them together with dogs— and not just dogs as pets, but dogs that will make a difference in somebody's life."

———— " ————

A few years later, Stoga heard about some newly developed programs that used prison inmates as puppy raisers. A veterinarian, Dr. Thomas Lane, started one of the first programs of this kind in Florida. Stoga also read a newspaper article about a similar program in Ohio. She was struck by the ways in which these programs could benefit the disabled and the inmates alike. "It made so much sense," she thought, "to have people who can give love, who have a lot of time, who need to be rehabilitated, and put them together with dogs— and not just dogs as pets, but dogs that will make a difference in somebody's life."

Stoga had some previous experience working for charitable causes. During the 1990s, for example, she served on New York City's Youth Empowerment Services Commission, which helped find jobs for low-income, inner-city teens. She eventually decided to draw on this experience to start her own dog-training program.

Founding Puppies Behind Bars

In July 1997 Stoga founded Puppies Behind Bars, a nonprofit organization dedicated to training prison inmates to serve as puppy raisers. A short time later, she received permission from Glenn Goord, the commissioner of the

New York Department of Corrections, to bring puppies into the state prison system for training.

But when Stoga approached Guiding Eyes for the Blind, a respected guide dog school and breeding facility in New York, she found that the organization was unwilling to provide her with dogs. "The initial reaction from all of the guide dog schools was: no way," she recalled. "I found myself in the position of having no guide dogs to bring to the prison." Some people felt that a prison was not an appropriate atmosphere for a puppy. Critics worried that the inmates would mistreat the dogs or train them to attack prison guards. Stoga understood these objections. In fact, she admitted that she held a negative view of prison inmates herself until she got to know them as people.

Stoga finally reached a compromise with Guiding Eyes for the Blind. To prove that her program could work, she arranged to buy five puppies that had failed to qualify for guide dog training and had been released from the school. In November 1997 she took these dogs to the Bedford Hills Correctional Facility—a maximum-security prison for women in upstate New York. If the inmates were able to train the puppies successfully, the school agreed to let Puppies Behind Bars raise qualified dogs. "Basically we had people that were written off by society raising dogs that were written off as potential guide dogs," Stoga noted.

As it turned out, the Puppies Behind Bars program was a huge success. Two of the first group of puppies qualified to become guide dogs for the blind, and the others went on to become working dogs in other capacities. "I have to say we were skeptical," said Jane Russenberger, director of breeding and placement for Guiding Eyes for the Blind. "The inmates at the Bedford prison have impressed me considerably. The work that they're doing and their commitment, the quality of the dogs that they're producing, the impeccable manners these dogs have—it's one of the finest puppy-raising jobs I've seen."

Stoga's early success paved the way for her to expand the program. Funded entirely by donations and staffed by volunteers, Puppies Behind Bars grew to include seven correctional facilities in three states over the next decade.

How the Program Works

When the puppies arrive at a prison, they are only eight weeks old. They are not yet housebroken and have not learned their names or any commands. Over the next 16 months, each puppy lives in a prison cell with its primary handler, who is responsible for providing it with basic care and af-

Inmates with their Labrador retriever puppies at the Fishkill Correctional Facility in New York. The inmates are listening to Stoga (off to the right, not shown), who is leading a class to train the dogs for guide work.

fection. Like other puppy raisers, the inmates also teach the puppies obedience and expose them to a variety of social situations. "The prison is a community unto itself," Stoga related. "These dogs go to the library, the dentist, chapel, the nursery, and offices within the prison where the inmates work each day."

Stoga also came up with ways for prison-raised puppies to experience the outside world. She organized a team of volunteer puppy sitters to take the dogs home with them on weekends and expose them to things they might encounter as working dogs, like crowds, traffic, sirens, shops, and restaurants. "Just going home to a person's apartment is different," Stoga explained. "Having rugs. Having sofas and chairs. Dishwashers, doorbells, coffee grinders. Everyday noises that aren't heard in prison." Stoga also started a program called Paws and Reflect, in which volunteers take puppies to visit elderly people who are confined to their homes. This experience helps the future service dogs get used to seeing wheelchairs, walkers, oxygen tanks, and hospital equipment.

Stoga chooses inmates to participate in the program carefully. She only considers those with spotless disciplinary records and at least two years remaining on their sentences. Interested inmates have to fill out an application and go through a screening process. Those selected as puppy raisers must attend classes on puppy training, complete homework assignments, and take tests. Stoga places a strong emphasis on the responsibility and commitment required to raise a puppy. "I ask them to fully understand what it is that they're doing, and if they can't handle the responsibility I ask them to leave," she explained. "I'm tough with them. I don't give them a lot of second and third chances. But I respect them, and I enjoy working with them."

> *Puppies changed the atmosphere at the medium-security men's prison, Fishkill Correctional Facility. According to deputy superintendent Jim Hayden, "The dogs have a calming, humanizing effect on the entire staff," he said. "They've broken these inmates down, taken their hard shells and cracked them open. Their level of love for and commitment to these dogs is something I never expected to see."*

Bonding with Prison Inmates

In addition to producing well-trained dogs for the disabled, Puppies Behind Bars also has a positive impact on the lives of the inmates. Participating in the program helps the inmates learn to express love, have patience, and accept responsibility. It also gives them increased self-esteem, a sense of purpose, and an opportunity to give something back to society. "Gloria saved my life," said Susan Hallett, an inmate serving a sentence of 25-years-to-life at Bedford Hills. "In prison it is so easy to slide into mental illness or to just give up. There are people who come along and don't realize they are life savers, but they are, and Gloria is one of them."

Jim Hayden, a deputy superintendent at Fishkill Correctional Facility in New York, noticed that Puppies Behind Bars changed the atmosphere at his medium-security men's prison. "The dogs have a calming, humanizing effect on the entire staff," he said. "They've broken these inmates down, taken their hard shells and cracked them open. Their level of love for and commitment to these dogs is something I never expected to see." Ronald Jones, a puppy raiser serving a 15-years-to-life sentence for murder at Fishkill, also witnessed a major change. "I've seen 6-foot-2, 250-pound guys rolling around on the floor kissing and talking in a high voice to their dogs," he noted. "We *all* do it, even in the yard with 200 other inmates and guards walking by. We don't care what anybody thinks. It's all about what's good for the dogs. We owe them. They did what nothing or nobody could—they took away our selfishness."

> "I've seen 6-foot-2, 250-pound guys rolling around on the floor kissing and talking in a high voice to their dogs," said Ronald Jones, a puppy raiser serving a 15-years-to-life sentence for murder. "We all do it, even in the yard with 200 other inmates and guards walking by. We don't care what anybody thinks. It's all about what's good for the dogs. We owe them. They did what nothing or nobody could—they took away our selfishness."

For the inmates who raise dogs for Puppies Behind Bars, the toughest part of the job is letting the dogs go after the 16 months of training are up. Some handlers take comfort in the fact that their dog will give a disabled person dignity, independence, and mobility. And some program participants find the bittersweet parting to be a valuable learning experience. "I felt what my mother must have felt on the day I was sentenced, when she stood next to the 24-year-old son she loved, who was going away for a long time," said inmate Thomas Lonetto of the moment when he said good-bye to the first dog he trained. "It's called empathy. I didn't know it existed in me until that moment."

For some inmates, the opportunity to train dogs for Puppies Behind Bars marks the first time anyone has trusted them or given them responsibility. Many participants in the program are inspired to study to become veterinary assistants or to earn bachelor's degrees. The program thus gives some participating inmates marketable skills to use upon their release from prison.

Inmates form a deep bond with the puppies they train, as shown by this pair at the Edna Mahan Correctional Facility in New Jersey.

"Most people can change," said former Bedford Hills superintendent Elaine Lord. "We need to give inmates meaningful work that will bring about that change—because most of them will get out, and our job is to make sure they aren't dangerous to society, but contributing members of society."

Changing People's Lives

In the years since she founded Puppies Behind Bars, Stoga has expanded its mission beyond training guide dogs for the blind. Following the terrorist attacks of September 11, 2001, the organization launched its Explosive Detection Canine Program. The inmates who participate in this program train dogs to assist law enforcement agencies by sniffing out bombs at airports, train stations, sporting events, and meeting places.

Paul Perricone, an officer with the New York Police Department's Bomb Squad, received an explosive detection dog named Sheeba from the Puppies Behind Bars program. Perricone visited the Edna Mahan Correctional Facility for Women in New Jersey to thank the inmates there for doing such a great job raising Sheeba. He explained how he depends on the dog to make the right decisions and keep him and other people safe. Sheeba has sniffed for bombs at a number of New York landmarks, including Yankee Stadium, the United Nations, and the U.S. Open tennis tournament. Two other explosive detection dogs raised by Puppies Behind Bars provide security for Egyptian president Hosni Mubarak.

——— " ———

"I felt what my mother must have felt on the day I was sentenced, when she stood next to the 24-year-old son she loved, who was going away for a long time," said inmate Thomas Lonetto of the moment when he said goodbye to the first dog he trained. "It's called empathy. I didn't know it existed in me until that moment."

——— 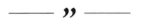 ———

In 2006 Stoga expanded Puppies Behind Bars to raise service dogs for adults and children with special needs, including autism and multiple sclerosis. The inmates teach the dogs 80 commands so that they can help disabled people perform such daily tasks as changing clothes, answering a telephone, opening a refrigerator, loading a washing machine, holding open a door, turning on a light switch, pushing an elevator button, or retrieving an item from a store shelf. As service dogs, they offer their disabled owners companionship, confidence, and independence.

Stoga also launched a program called Dog Tags: Service Dogs for Those Who've Served Us. This element of Puppies Behind Bars provides service dogs to U.S. military veterans of the wars in Afghanistan and Iraq. The dogs can assist veterans who have suffered physical injuries, traumatic brain injuries, or Post-Traumatic Stress Disorder (PTSD, a condition characterized by extreme fear and anxiety that develops following exposure to a severe emotional or physical trauma).

The first dog to come out of the Dog Tags program, Pax, was paired with Sergeant William Campbell, an Iraq War veteran with PTSD. Once too frightened by flashbacks and nightmares to leave his home in Washington State, Campbell felt secure enough to bring Pax across the country to thank the women who raised him at Bedford Hills. "As inmates, we can understand the loss of freedom," said Jaymie Powers, a puppy raiser who is serving a sentence for murder. "Through these dogs we can give someone a chance at freedom."

HOME AND FAMILY

Stoga lives in New York City. She is married and has two adult children.

FURTHER READING

Periodicals

Christian Science Monitor, Aug. 16, 2000, p.15
Good Housekeeping, Apr. 2001, p.88
New York Times, Aug. 22, 1999, p.1; June 9, 2004, Metro, p.1; June 1, 2008, p.WE1; Nov. 30, 2008, p.WE1
Saturday Evening Post, Sep. 1, 2005, p.64
Smithsonian, Aug. 2004, p.62

Online Articles

http://www.bloomberg.com
(Bloomberg.com, "Maimed U.S. War Veterans Find Freedom with Prison-Raised Dogs," Nov. 18, 2008)

ADDRESS

Gloria Gilbert Stoga
Puppies Behind Bars
10 East 40th Street
19th Floor
New York, NY 10016

WORLD WIDE WEB SITE

http://www.puppiesbehindbars.com

Shailene Woodley 1991-

American Actress

Star of "The Secret Life of the American Teenager"

BIRTH

Shailene Diann Woodley was born on November 15, 1991, in Simi Valley, California. Her mother, Lori, works as a middle school counselor. Her father, Loni, is a school principal. She has one younger brother, Tanner.

YOUTH AND EDUCATION

Woodley was born and raised in Simi Valley, a prosperous middle-class community in the metropolitan Los Angeles area. Her childhood featured the usual bumps and scrapes, but her parents provided a loving and nurturing home for both of their children. As Woodley herself said, "I feel fortunate to have grown up in a safe and family-oriented environment."

Woodley's acting career began when she was only five years old. "It was kind of an accident, actually," she recalled. "I'm not even entirely sure how it happened. My cousin used to be a model and one day brought a talent-call audition thing with her and my mom was like, 'Hey, you want to act today?' and I was like, 'Sure!' And it just kind of happened. I was never forced to do it, and I never forced them to take me to auditions. It was just kind of one of those things that worked for everybody."

Woodley was thrilled when she began appearing on television in small roles. But she still had plenty of time to be a regular kid. She attended neighborhood public schools all the way through high school, and she never really felt different from her friends. "[Acting has] just been my hobby," she explained. "My friends went to soccer practice; I went to auditions." Her parents also made sure that she kept a level head about her acting career. "I had rules," she said. "I had to stay the person I knew I was. I had to stay really respectful [of my parents] … and I had to still do good in school."

> "[Acting has] just been my hobby," she explained. "My friends went to soccer practice; I went to auditions." Her parents also made sure that she kept a level head about her acting career. "I had rules," she said. "I had to stay the person I knew I was. I had to stay really respectful [of my parents] … and I had to still do good in school."

Dealing with Scoliosis

By the time Woodley reached high school, her acting roles were getting more demanding and exciting. But her mid-teens were filled with pain and disappointment in other ways. When she was a freshman her parents got divorced, and when she was 15 she was diagnosed with scoliosis, a potentially dangerous curvature of the spine.

Woodley remembered when she got her first clue that she suffered from scoliosis. "We were getting ready to go swimming and I was in a bikini," she recalled, when suddenly her best friend said, "Shai, your spine is

FULL-LENGTH MOVIE

*One of Woodley's first big roles was in the
TV movie* Felicity *from the* American Girl *series.*

weird." What her friend had noticed was that Woodley's spine had an abnormal curve to it. She was quickly rushed off to see doctors, who reassured Woodley and her parents that she would be fine with treatment.

Woodley's doctors explained that scoliosis affects roughly two percent of the population and that most cases do not even require medical treatment. The doctors acknowledged that Woodley's condition would require intervention. But they assured her that she would not have to undergo surgery, which is required in cases where scoliosis threatens to cause severe deformities or damage heart and lung functions. Instead, she would be outfitted in a chest-to-hips plastic brace to straighten her spine.

Woodley spent most of the next two years in the brace. She did not have to wear it when she swam, went out with her friends, or was filming. But she was required to keep the brace on at virtually all other times—an average of 18 hours a day. The situation quickly became frustrating for the energetic youth. By the fourth week of wearing the brace, she found herself repeatedly thinking, "Whoa, this is a bummer." But she accepted the treatment as necessary, and she was able to take the brace off for good in December 2008, a few months before her graduation from high school.

CAREER HIGHLIGHTS

Woodley's first few parts on television were very small. In 2002, though, she won guest starring roles in the crime dramas "Without a Trace" and "The District." Her strong performances in these parts led to appearances over the next few years on several other popular TV series, including "Everybody Loves Raymond," "My Name Is Earl," "CSI: New York," and "Cold Case." Woodley also earned a recurring role in two series during this period. She played the character of Kaitlin Cooper in the 2003 season of "The O.C.," and from 2001 to 2004 she made four different appearances in the drama "Crossing Jordan" as the childhood version of the title character.

Woodley's biggest roles during her early teen years, though, came in two made-for-television films. In 2004 she had a significant part in a Hallmark Channel movie called *A Place Called Home*, starring Ann-Margret. One year later, she made an even bigger splash as the title character in the TV movie *Felicity: An American Girl Adventure*. In this film, which was inspired by the popular line of children's dolls, Woodley played a brave young girl in colonial America. The plot centers around her decision to rescue a beautiful wild horse that is being cruelly mistreated by its owner.

Felicity received praise for delivering positive messages to young girls about the importance of kindness and standing up for your beliefs. "*Felicity* is high adventure for its young target audience," said a reviewer for the *Hollywood Reporter.* "[It] makes history come alive in a compelling way for young viewers."

"The Secret Life of the American Teenager"

Woodley's strong performance in *Felicity* and on various TV shows caught the attention of executives at the ABC Family network. They asked her to audition for the starring role in a new series they were preparing called "The Secret Life of the American Teenager." Woodley's impressive audition convinced producers that she was ideal for the part, and in February 2008 they announced that she had won the role.

In "Secret Life," Woodley plays the part of Amy Juergens, a generally smart, cheerful, and responsible 15-year-old girl. Amy's life changes radically when she impulsively has sex for the first time at band camp with a "cool" older boy from her high school, then finds out that she is pregnant. She decides to keep the baby, but fights through feelings of confusion and fear as the pregnancy progresses. "She's a go-getter, she's excited for life, she wants to go to Juilliard, she has all these amazing goals," explained Woodley. "And then she finds out she's pregnant, and her world kind of comes crashing down and her sense of optimism turns to pessimism. And she freaks out, because all she's ever known has been completely turned upside down."

Woodley's character serves as the focal point of a wider story about the trials and tribulations of a group of middle-class high school students and their families. As the first season unfolded, viewers also got to know other characters such as Amy's mother, played by former teen movie star Molly Ringwald. But the action always returns to Amy and her relationships with the father of her child, played by Daren Kagasoff, and her current boyfriend, played by Ken Baumann.

When "Secret Life" first arrived on TV screens in 2008, critics were divid-

"She's a go-getter, she's excited for life, she wants to go to Juilliard, she has all these amazing goals," Woodley said about her character, Amy Juergens. *"And then she finds out she's pregnant, and her world kind of comes crashing down and her sense of optimism turns to pessimism. And she freaks out, because all she's ever known has been completely turned upside down."*

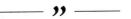

163

Scenes from "The Secret Life of the American Teenager."

ed about the show. The *New York Times* dismissed "Secret Life" as predictable and silly and said that the show "doesn't take the fun out of teenage pregnancy; it takes the fun out of television." The *San Francisco Chronicle,* on the other hand, said that the show "makes an effort to discuss some of the real challenges that would face any family of a pregnant teenager." The reviewer added that "Shailene Woodley and Ken Baumann are sweet and believably scared about the future as Amy and Ben."

As the reviews poured in, about the only thing that critics agreed about was that Woodley delivered a terrific and sympathetic portrayal of Amy. "Woodley is cute in an everyday way, and her shyness and visible thought processes are very endearing," declared one North Carolina newspaper. "Instantly, she's someone to root for, as she considers the consequences of her options." *Entertainment Weekly,* meanwhile, stated that "like a great silent-film actress, [Woodley] has a face that conveys shades of anguish and joy. Her performance lifts a well-meaning, rather brave, but ramshackle show a notch."

——— *"* ———

"[I've] heard a lot of teenage girls say they like how the script talks about high school drama because it is happening in real life," Woodley said. *"There are so many different aspects of life that it definitely dives into and I thought that was really interesting to be able to portray that to ... America's teenagers and teenagers all over the world and [say that] you're not alone."*

Enjoying a Hit Series

By the end of the first season, it was clear that TV viewers did not care about the show's mixed critical reception. "Secret Life" was a big hit, especially with teenagers and their families. According to Woodley, the show's popularity is easy to understand. "[I've] heard a lot of teenage girls say they like how the script talks about high school drama because it is happening in real life," she said. "There are so many different aspects of life that it definitely dives into and I thought that was really interesting to be able to portray that to ... America's teenagers and teenagers all over the world and [say that] you're not alone.... Everyone goes through trials and tribulations as a teenager and this is how we're dealing with it."

Woodley also rejects criticism from a few reviewers about the way that "Secret Life" depicts teen pregnancy. "I don't feel like this show glorifies

> "
>
> *"I don't feel like this show glorifies pregnancy, because if you see my character she's obviously not jumping up and down, she's in the bathroom crying 24/7," Woodley explained. "If anything, I think it makes it seem like a very hard and difficult situation to go through, especially as a teenager."*
>
> "

pregnancy, because if you see my character she's obviously not jumping up and down, she's in the bathroom crying 24/7," she said. "If anything, I think it makes it seem like a very hard and difficult situation to go through, especially as a teenager."

Woodley is proud of the show, and she knows that Ringwald and the rest of the actors, writers, and crew on "Secret Life" feel the same way. She also loves the atmosphere on the set of the show. "Everyone is so great and everyone gets along so well," she said. "We're all so close and we have kinds of things like parties and dinners for each other for our birthdays and we all kind of play guitar, so we're always jamming in the trailers. It's a fun environment."

Playing the Role of Amy

Ever since "Secret Life" debuted, interviewers and fans have expressed curiosity about Woodley's view of the character she plays. She admits that "it's tricky sometimes because there are things that Amy does that I'm like, 'Why would she do this?' I just have to accept it and go along with it and find ways to make it work and find ways to believe it for myself, even though I would never even tell a boy I loved him at 15."

Woodley enjoys the challenge of playing someone so different from herself, though. "This is my first role where she's basically sad and lost in tragedy but still a teenager, still excited about school dances, and she has a new boyfriend, and she's finding love for the first time," she explained. "So it's a bunch of different colors that I kind of have to put into one rainbow, so it's been fun to figure out."

Woodley also believes that the role has allowed her to grow as an actress, because Amy has changed over the course of the show's existence. "I feel like she's become much stronger, personality-wise," she said. "She's learned to accept the fact that life isn't going to be perfect and that there are going to be many, many obstacles that she has to go through throughout her life…. I don't mean to discount the fact that she's still hurting and

Fans of "Secret Life" have been glad to see the characters grow and develop over multiple seasons.

crying and emotionally stricken by the whole situation, but she's just accepted that it's going to have to happen. I think there's a state of acceptance and she's become stronger."

Adjusting to Stardom

"The Secret Life of the American Teenager" has changed Woodley's life in other ways as well. She enjoys interacting with fans, for example, but admits that it still feels strange to be the subject of fan web sites and to be identified by *Entertainment Weekly* as a "breakout star." "It's definitely different," she said. "When you go to a grocery store and you go anywhere there are people staring or pointing or whispering, and every now and then you have a brave girl come up and be like, 'Are you the girl from 'Secret Life'?'"

Woodley insists, though, that her growing stardom has not changed her personality or values. "As far as just my friends and where I can go, I still go all the places that I normally went. I might have to wear a hat or something [to disguise myself], but other than that it's no different because my friends, they treat me the same. They know I'm goofy, spontaneous, weird Shai and they accept me for that."

> *"There are so many emotions that you go through, whether it's when you're going through puberty and you have all these hormones ... or whether it's a breakup with the boyfriend or divorcing parents," Woodley advised. "Just stay strong and remain who you are because the only thing that will keep you in check and keep you the person that everybody knows and loves is if you stay true to yourself ... and know that you're super special."*

Woodley also believes that she can use her high profile to help teenage fans going through their own turmoil. She urges teen girls to be brave and trust in themselves when life throws obstacles in their way. "There are so many emotions that you go through, whether it's when you're going through puberty and you have all these hormones going through your mind and you don't even know what to think, or whether it's a breakup with the boyfriend or divorcing parents," Woodley advised. "Just stay strong and remain who you are because the only thing that will keep you in check and keep you the person that everybody knows and loves is if you stay true to yourself ... and know that you're super special."

Woodley describes acting as a "passion" and wants to continue with that career. But she also has many other plans for her future. For example, she would like to go to college in

New York City or someplace else on the East Coast "where it's cold and where you actually get seasons." She is particularly interested in studying psychology and interior design. "They're completely opposite [subjects]," she admits, "but I'm creative and I love the arts, so that's why I like interior design; and I think psychology is just so fascinating to be able to study the human mind and the human characteristics and the way they work. So I think that's definitely up my alley. I want to have options."

HOME AND FAMILY

Woodley lives in California, where "Secret Life" is filmed. She remains close to both her mother and father.

HOBBIES AND OTHER INTERESTS

Woodley has a wide range of interests that she likes to pursue when she is not on the set. She likes camping, hiking, Pilates, and painting, and she loves to sew. "I love to make bags or shirts or dresses or whatever," she said. After a tiring day of filming, though, she admits that she also enjoys just watching television with friends or family. "If I'm super exhausted, nothing soothes me better than 'Top Chef' or 'Project Runway,'" she stated.

SELECTED CREDITS

A Place Called Home, 2004
Felicity: An American Girl Adventure, 2005
"The Secret Life of the American Teenager," 2008- (ongoing)

FURTHER READING

Periodicals

Boston Herald, Jan. 5, 2009, p.27
Entertainment Weekly, Aug. 8, 2008, p.53; Nov. 21, 2008, p.86; Jan. 9, 2009, p.32
Girls Life, Aug.-Sep. 2008, p.48
Hollywood Reporter, Nov. 29, 2005, p.32
New York Times, July 1, 2008, p.E1
People, Jan. 26, 2009, p.42
Raleigh (NC) News & Observer, Aug. 10, 2008
San Francisco Chronicle, Jan. 3, 2009, p.E1
USA Today, June 30, 2008, p.D6

Online Articles

http://www.sidereel.com
> (Sidereel.com, "New Media Strategies: The Secret Life of the American Teenager—Shailene Woodley Q&A," Dec. 29, 2008)

http://www.tvaholic.com
> (TVaholic.com, "Interview with Shailene Woodley," July 7, 2008)

http://www.webmd.com
> (WebMD.com, "Actress Shailene Woodley Takes Scoliosis in Stride," no date)

ADDRESS

Shailene Woodley
"The Secret Life of the American Teenager" ABC Family
500 South Buena Vista Street
Burbank, CA 91521

WORLD WIDE WEB SITES

http://www.abcfamily.com
http://www.myspace.com/ishailenewoodley
http://www.shailene-woodley.com

Photo and Illustration Credits

Front Cover Photos: Joe Biden: U.S. Army photo by K. Kassens; Jimmie Johnson: Matthew T. Thacker/Landov; Michelle Obama: Official portrait of First Lady Michelle Obama/WhiteHouse.gov; Shailene Woodley: ABC Family/Craig Sjodin.

Will Allen/Photos: Courtesy of Growing Power, Inc. (pp. 9, 12, 15, 17).

Judy Baca/Photos: Portrait of artist Judith F. Baca at the "Great Wall of Los Angeles," 2005 © SPARC www.sparcmurals.org (p. 21); Artist Judith F. Baca with mural crew at the "Great Wall of Los Angeles," 1983 © SPARC www.sparcmurals.org (p. 24); "MI ABUELITA" 1970, 20 ft. x 35 ft. Acrylic on cement. © SPARC www.sparc murals.org (p. 27); "GREAT WALL OF LOS ANGELES" begun 1976. DETAIL: A view of the 13' x 2,400' "Great Wall" mural located in the Tujunga Wash, a flood control channel. The World's longest mural depicts a multi-cultural history of California from prehistory through to the 1950's. This mural is still growing. The Great Wall is located in California's San Fernando Valley Tujunga Wash, a flood control channel built in the 1930's. Acrylic on cast concrete, summer 1983. © SPARC www.sparc murals.org (p. 29); "WORLD WALL: A Vision of the Future Without Fear" begun 1990. DETAIL: "WORLD WALL" installation in Mexico City 2006, eight panels totaling 10' x 240' acrylic on canvas. Begun in 1990, the World Wall is an international traveling mural installation consisting of numerous transportable panels with the theme "a vision of the future without fear." The completed work consists of eight 10' x 30' portable murals that bring forth a spiritual and material transformation of an individual, a community, and a nation towards peace. The World Wall had its premiere in Joensuu, Finland, and traveled to Gorky Park, Moscow, USSR, in the summer of 1990 and continues to travel to new countries every year. © SPARC www. sparcmurals.org (p. 32); THE CESAR E. CHAVEZ MONUMENT "ARCH OF DIGNITY, EQUALITY AND JUSTICE" DETAIL: "Arch of Dignity, Equality and Justice," 2008. The Cesar E. Chavez monument at San Jose State University consists of farm workers featured in two murals painted and printed digitally, a portrait of Cesar Chavez painted and then produced in full color Venetian tile, along with portraits of Gandhi and Dolores Huerta. The monument at San Jose State University in San Jose, California, was designed by Judith F. Baca and the UCLA/SPARC Cesar Chavez Digital Mural Lab. The monument commemorates Chavez through his ideals and beliefs, carried out in his actions to improve the conditions of the campesino, which inspired so many to join his efforts to achieve social justice. © SPARC www.sparcmurals.org (p. 35).

Joe Biden/Photos: U.S. Army photo by K. Kassens (p. 39); Book cover: PROMISES TO KEEP (Random House) Copyright © 2007 by Joseph Biden. All Rights Reserved. Cover photo by Luigi Ciuffetelli. Cover design by David Stevenson. (p. 41); AP

Photo (p. 44); Antonio Dickey, photographer. Chicago Public Library, Special Collections and Preservation Division, HWAC 1987-5-11 (p. 47); AP Photo/Barry Thumma (p. 49); Paul J. Richards/AFP/Getty Images (p. 50); Department of Defense photo by Master Sgt. Cecilio Ricardo/U.S. Air Force (p. 52).

Lupe Fiasco/Photos: NBC photo/Dave Bjerke (p. 57); Saverio Truglia/WireImage (p. 59); CD Cover: LUPE FIASCO'S FOOD & LIQUOR Copyright © Warner Elektra Atlantic Corporation (p. 63); Copyright © Warner Elektra Atlantic Corporation. Photo by Ray Tamarrra (p. 66); Tim Mosenfelder/Getty Images (p. 68).

James Harrison/Photos: AP Photo/John Bazemore (p. 71); Courtesy of Kent State Athletic Communications (p. 73); AP Photo/Jack Smith (p. 76); Andy Lyons/Getty Images (p. 78); Mark Cornelison/MCT/Landov (p. 81).

Jimmie Johnson/Photos: AP Photo/Glenn Smith (p. 85); AP Photo/Mark J. Terrill (p. 88); AP Photo/Wilfredo Lee (p. 91); AP Photo/J. Pat Carter (p. 93); Doug Benc/Getty Images (p. 96); AP Photo/Paul Connors (p. 99).

Demi Lovato/Photos: Disney Channel/Nick Ray (p. 103); Barney & Friends ™, Courtesy of PBS KIDS Sprout/via Comcast (p. 104); DVD: CAMP ROCK: EXTENDED ROCK STAR EDITION, 2008. Copyright © Disney. All Rights Reserved. (p. 108, top and center); Disney Channel/Heidi Gutman (p. 108, bottom); TV: SONNY WITH A CHANCE. Disney Channel/Randy Holmes (p. 111); TV: PRINCESS PROTECTION PROGRAM, Disney Channel/Francisco Roman (p. 112).

Michelle Obama/Photos: Official portrait of First Lady Michelle Obama/WhiteHouse.gov (p. 115); AP Photo/Obama for America (p. 118); Courtesy/University of Chicago (p. 120); AP Photo/Charlie Neibergall (p. 124); Department of Defense photo by Master Sgt. Gerold Gamble/U.S. Air Force (p. 127); The White House/Joyce N. Boghosian (p. 130, top); Courtesy of Corporation for National and Community Service. Photo by M.T. Harmon, Office of Public Affairs. (p. 130, center). Official White House Photo by Samantha Appleton (p. 130, bottom).

Robert Pattinson/Photos: Elisabetta A. Villa/WireImage.com (p. 135); Movie stills: HARRY POTTER AND THE GOBLET OF FIRE. Copyright © 2006 Warner Bros Entertainment. Publishing rights © J. K. Rowling. Harry Potter characters, names, and related indicia are trademarks of and © Warner Bros Entertainment. All Rights Reserved. (p. 138, top, center and bottom); Movie still: TWILIGHT © Summit Entertainment/Peter Sorel (p. 140); Picture Group/MTV (p. 143); Movie still: HOW TO BE Copyright © 2009 How To Films Ltd. (p. 145).

Gloria Gilbert Stoga/Photos: Courtesy/Puppies Behind Bars. Photo by Keith Barraclough (p. 149); AP Photo/Jim McKnight (p. 152); AP Photo/Daniel Hulshizer (p. 155).

Shailene Woodley/Photos: ABC Family/Bob D'Amico (p. 159); DVD cover: FELICITY: AN AMERICAN GIRL ADVENTURE. American Girl, Felicity, Felicity Merriman and the associated characters and trademarks of The American Girl Collection are owned by American Girl, LLC. Package design, supplementary material compilation and distribution © 2005 Warner Bros Entertainment Inc. All Rights Reserved. (p. 161); ABC Family/Bob D'Amico (p. 164, top); ABC Family/Craig Sjodin (p. 164, center); ABC Family/Randy Holmes (p. 164, bottom); DVD: THE SECRET LIFE OF THE AMERICAN TEENAGER: SEASON 2 Copyright © WDSHE. All Rights Reserved. (p. 167).

Cumulative Names Index

This cumulative index includes the names of all individuals profiled in *Biography Today* since the debut of the series in 1992.

For cumulative general, places of birth, and birthday indexes, please see biographytoday.com.

For cumulative general, places of birth, and birthday indexes, please see biographytoday.com.

175

For cumulative general, places of birth, and birthday indexes, please see biographytoday.com.

177

For cumulative general, places of birth, and birthday indexes, please see biographytoday.com.

179

For cumulative general, places of birth, and birthday indexes, please see biographytoday.com.

181

For cumulative general, places of birth, and birthday indexes, please see biographytoday.com.

For cumulative general, places of birth, and birthday indexes, please see biographytoday.com.

185

For cumulative general, places of birth, and birthday indexes, please see biographytoday.com.

For cumulative general, places of birth, and birthday indexes, please see biographytoday.com.

187

For cumulative general, places of birth, and birthday indexes, please see biographytoday.com.

For cumulative general, places of birth, and birthday indexes, please see biographytoday.com.

189